Enough Already! A Workbook to Eliminate Negative Thinking

A Step-by-Step Guide With 24 Powerful Exercises to Let Go of Self-Doubt, Manage Anxiety, Build Confidence, and Love Yourself

Mimi Wingo

© **Copyright 2025 - All rights reserved.**

The content contained within this book may not be reproduced, duplicated or transmitted without direct written permission from the author or the publisher.

Under no circumstances will any blame or legal responsibility be held against the publisher, or author, for any damages, reparation, or monetary loss due to the information contained within this book, either directly or indirectly.

Legal Notice:

This book is copyright protected. It is only for personal use. You cannot amend, distribute, sell, use, quote or paraphrase any part, or the content within this book, without the consent of the author or publisher.

Disclaimer Notice:

Please note the information contained within this document is for educational and entertainment purposes only. All effort has been executed to present accurate, up to date, reliable, complete information. No warranties of any kind are declared or implied. Readers acknowledge that the author is not engaged in the rendering of legal, financial, medical or professional advice. The content within this book has been derived from various sources. Please consult a licensed professional before attempting any techniques outlined in this book.

By reading this document, the reader agrees that under no circumstances is the author responsible for any losses, direct or indirect, that are incurred as a result of the use of the information contained within this document, including, but not limited to, errors, omissions, or inaccuracies.

Table of Contents

INTRODUCTION 1

CHAPTER 1: UNDERSTANDING THE ROOTS OF NEGATIVE SELF-TALK 5

IDENTIFY PERSONAL TRIGGERS AND THEIR ORIGINS 5
EXERCISE: IDENTIFYING SPECIFIC SITUATIONS OF NEGATIVE SELF-TALK 7
    Reflect and Write..*7*
    Set the Scene..*8*
    Notice Your Thoughts...*9*
    Identify Triggers...*9*
    Coping Strategies...*10*
    Regular Check-Ins..*10*
JOURNAL EXERCISE TO UNCOVER TRIGGER PATTERNS..11
    Daily Journaling...*11*
    Trigger Tracking Grid...*11*
HOW TO USE THE GRID..13
    Prompting Reflection...*13*
    Monthly Review...*16*
DEVELOP A PLAN TO TRACK AND MANAGE TRIGGERS...16
    Setting Realistic Goals...*17*
    Reflection and Revision...*18*

CHAPTER 2: HOW TO IDENTIFY AND CHALLENGE YOUR INNER CRITIC 21

STRATEGY FOR ACKNOWLEDGING AND DIALOGUING WITH YOUR INNER CRITIC................21
    Understanding Your Inner Critic..*22*
    Engaging in Constructive Dialogue..*22*
EXERCISE: ENGAGING IN CONSTRUCTIVE DIALOGUE WITH YOUR INNER CRITIC..............23
    Set the Scene..*24*
    Identify Your Inner Critic...*24*
    Initiate a Dialogue...*25*
    Ask Questions...*25*
    Practice Compassion...*26*
    Establish Boundaries...*26*
    Reflect on the Conversation..*27*
    Regular Practice..*28*
    Reframing Your Inner Dialogue...*28*
EXERCISE: REFRAMING YOUR INNER DIALOGUE FOR EMPOWERMENT.............................30
    Identify Negative Phrases..*30*

- *Transform the Dialogue* 30
- *Create Anchor Phrases* 31
- *Practice Rescripting* 31
- *Emphasize Self-Compassion* 32
- *Repeat and Reinforce* 33
- *Reflect on the Impact* 33

PERSONIFICATION OF YOUR INNER CRITIC 34
- *Dialogue With the Persona* 34
- *Evaluating the Persona's Arguments* 35
- *Changing the Character* 36

EXERCISE: PERSONIFICATION OF YOUR INNER CRITIC 36
- *Creating a Critic Persona* 36
- *Evaluate the Persona's Arguments* 40
- *Transforming the Character* 41

TECHNIQUE FOR TRANSFORMING CRITICAL THOUGHTS 45
- *Recognizing Automatic Negative Thoughts* 45
- *Reframing and Replacing Negative Thoughts* 46

EXERCISE: TRANSFORMING CRITICAL THOUGHTS INTO POSITIVE AFFIRMATIONS ... 46
- *Recognizing ANTs* 47
- *Understanding Triggers* 47
- *Recognizing Patterns* 48
- *Crafting Positive Affirmations* 48
- *Daily Affirmation Practice* 49
- *Response Preparation* 49
- *Reflection* 49

CHAPTER 3: REWRITING YOUR INNER NARRATIVE 51

CRAFTING UNIQUE POSITIVE AFFIRMATIONS 51
- *Affirmation Practice* 52
- *Making Them Yours* 52

EXERCISE: CREATING PERSONAL AFFIRMATIONS 53
- *Understand the Challenge* 53
- *Personalize Your Affirmations* 55
- *Experiment With Formulations* 56
- *Establish an Affirmation Practice* 57
- *Share With Friends* 58
- *Evaluating Effectiveness* 58

IMPLEMENTING VISUALIZATION TECHNIQUES 59

EXERCISE: GUIDED VISUALIZATION FOR CHALLENGING NEGATIVE BELIEFS 61
- *Find Your Space* 61
- *Set an Intention* 61
- *Incorporate Sensory Details* 63
- *Embrace the Emotions* 64
- *Affirm Your Experience* 65

Regular Practice 65
Journal Your Thoughts 65
CREATING VISION BOARDS 66
EXERCISE: INCORPORATING AFFIRMATIONS AND VISUALIZATIONS INTO YOUR
DAILY ROUTINE 67
Recognize the Importance of Consistency 67
Build a Daily Practice 68
Start Small 68
Create a Supportive Environment 69
Track Your Progress 69
Stay Flexible 70
Celebrate Your Wins 71
EXERCISE: TRACKING YOUR PROGRESS IN EMOTIONAL GROWTH 71
Start a Journaling Practice 71
Identify Patterns and Trends 71
Utilize App Technology 72
Celebrate Small Victories 72
Reflect on Your Growth 72
Share Your Journey 73

CHAPTER 4: BUILDING UNSHAKEABLE SELF-ESTEEM 76

EXPLANATION OF RESILIENCE-BUILDING METHODS 76
EXERCISE: BUILDING RESILIENCE THROUGH PRACTICAL STRATEGIES 78
Identify Your Challenges 78
Problem-Solving Practice 79
Develop a Support Network 80
Connection Idea 81
Cultivate a Growth Mindset 82
Embrace Challenges 82
Daily Resilience Practice 83
Reflect on Progress 83
THE ROLE OF MINDSET 85
The Magic of a Positive Mindset 85
Resilience in Action 86
THE POWER OF GRATITUDE JOURNALING 87
What Is Gratitude Journaling? 87
The Benefits of Gratitude 88
EXERCISE: STARTING YOUR GRATITUDE JOURNAL 90
Gather Your Supplies 90
Set a Consistent Time 90
Start With Simple Prompts 91
Note Big and Small Things 91
Reflect on Your Entries 91
Explore Sharing Gratitude 93

Positive Effects of Sharing 93
Reflect on Relationships 93
Collective Gratitude 93
UTILIZING POSITIVE SELF-REFLECTION FOR SELF-ESTEEM ENHANCEMENT 94
What Is Positive Self-Reflection? 94
EXERCISE: METHODS FOR EFFECTIVE SELF-REFLECTION 95
Set the Stage for Reflection 95
End-of-Day Review 95
Set Specific Reflection Goals 96
Daily Journaling 97
Practice Mindfulness 97
Weekly Reflection Sessions 98
Recognize Growth 98
Share Reflections With a Trusted Friend 98

CHAPTER 5: THE CONFIDENCE MINDSET **99**

DIFFERENTIATING CONFIDENCE FROM COMPETENCE 99
Defining Confidence 99
Understanding Competence 100
The Interplay Between Confidence and Competence 100
EXERCISE: CULTIVATING CONFIDENCE AND COMPETENCE 101
Define Your Goals 101
Set Incremental Steps 103
Seek Out Challenges 104
Document Your Experiences 104
Reflect on Past Successes 105
Create a Confidence Board 105
Celebrate Your Journey 106
Establish a Supportive Network 106
PRACTICING THE POWER POSE 106
Practical Instructions for Power Posing 108
The Science Behind It 108
Incorporating Power Posing Into Daily Life 109
REWRITING NEGATIVE THOUGHTS INTO EMPOWERING STATEMENTS 110
The Impact of Reframed Thoughts 110
EXERCISE: BUILDING A HABIT OF REFRAMING NEGATIVE THOUGHTS 112
Establish a Routine 112
Create Daily Affirmations 113
Integrate Gratitude 113
Combine Practices 113
Track Your Progress 115
Set Monthly Check-Ins 115

CHAPTER 6: OVERCOMING THE FEAR OF JUDGMENT 117

EVOLUTIONARY AND PERSONAL ROOTS OF THE FEAR OF JUDGMENT 117
  Personal Experiences: Stories That Stick 118
  The Power of Narratives: Rewriting Your Story 119
JOURNALING TO IDENTIFY JUDGMENT PATTERNS 119
  Creating a Judgment Journal: A Tool for Awareness 119
  Prompting Reflection: Asking the Right Questions 120
  Reviewing Patterns: Spotting the Recurring Themes 120
  Visualization Techniques: Adding Depth to Reflection 121
EXERCISE: JOURNALING TO IDENTIFY JUDGMENT PATTERNS 122
  Create a Judgment Journal 122
  Acknowledge Feelings in Real Time 123
  Document Specific Situations 123
  Utilize Targeted Reflection Prompts 123
  Analyze Your Responses 124
  Regularly Review Patterns 124
  Incorporate Visualization Techniques 125
METHODS OF SELF-EVALUATION FOR PERSONAL JUDGMENTS 125
  Self-Assessment Techniques: Getting Clear on the Inner Critic 125
EXERCISE: CREATING A JUDGMENT DETOX PLAN 126
  Understanding Self-Judgment 126
  Identify Your Triggers 127
  Create Compassionate Alternatives 129
  Develop Strategies for Reduction 129
  Create a Commitment Statement 130
  Implement your Judgment Detox Plan 131
  Regular Check-Ins 131
  Celebrate Progress 132
POSITIVE AFFIRMATION ALTERNATIVES: FLIPPING THE SCRIPT 133
SEEKING EXTERNAL FEEDBACK: SEEING YOURSELF THROUGH KINDER EYES 133

CHAPTER 7: BREAKING FREE FROM THE CYCLE OF OVERTHINKING 135

KEEPING A GRATITUDE JOURNAL FOR POSITIVE REINFORCEMENT 135
  Daily Gratitude Practices 136
EXERCISE: DAILY GRATITUDE PRACTICES 137
  Incorporate Daily Gratitude Prompts 137
  Morning Gratitude Routine 138
  Evening Reflections 138
  Transforming Overthinking With Gratitude 140
  Writing for Mental Reset 141
  The Power of Sharing Gratitude 141
  Deepening Connections Through Sharing 141
  Encourage Collective Gratitude 143

MEDITATION AS A TOOL FOR MENTAL CLARITY 143
   Creating a Consistent Practice *144*
  EXERCISE: SIMPLE MEDITATION TECHNIQUES FOR BEGINNERS 144
   Start With Breathing Exercises *144*
   Explore Guided Meditation Apps *145*
   Incorporate Visualization Techniques *145*
   Understand Mindfulness in Addressing Overthinking *145*
   Practice Presence *146*
   Create a Consistent Meditation Practice *146*
   Track Your Progress *146*

CHAPTER 8: MINDFULNESS AND LIVING IN THE PRESENT 149

  SUNLIGHT VISUALIZATION FOR STRESS RELIEF 149
  EXERCISE: SUNLIGHT VISUALIZATION FOR STRESS RELIEF 150
   Understanding Sunlight Visualization *150*
   Creating Your Calm Space *151*
   Visualizing the Sunlight *151*
   Fostering Warmth and Safety *151*
   Breathing With the Sunlight *151*
   Implementing the Technique Into Daily Routines *152*
   A Reminder of Positivity *152*
   Reflect on Your Experience *152*
   Benefits of Regular Practice *153*
   Personal Reflection on the Experience *153*
  NOTING MEDITATION TECHNIQUE 154
  EXERCISE: NOTING MEDITATION TECHNIQUE 155
   Setting the Scene *155*
   Establishing a Time Frame *156*
   Begin With Your Breath *156*
   Start Noting *156*
   Recognize Patterns *157*
   Adjusting the Practice *157*
   Concluding the Practice *158*
   Daily Integration *158*
   Benefits of Noting Meditation *158*
   Encouraging Regular Practice *159*

CHAPTER 9: EMBRACING VULNERABILITY AND AUTHENTICITY 162

  EXPLORING THE CONCEPT OF EMOTIONAL EXPOSURE 163
   The Benefits of Vulnerability *163*
   Cultural Perspectives on Vulnerability *164*
   Sharing Personal Stories *164*
  SELF-ACCEPTANCE EXERCISES TO BUILD CONFIDENCE 164
   Affirmation Practices *165*

Why Affirmations Work..*165*
EXERCISE: SELF-ACCEPTANCE EXERCISES TO BUILD CONFIDENCE *166*
   Understanding Self-Acceptance *166*
   Create Personal Affirmations *167*
   Customize Your Affirmations..*168*
   Daily Affirmation Practice *170*
   Track Your Progress..*170*
   Embrace Vulnerability *170*
   Practice Self-Compassion *172*
   Celebrate Your Journey..*172*
EXERCISE: SELF-COMPASSION TECHNIQUES...*172*
   Understanding Self-Compassion *172*
   Kindness to Yourself *173*
   The Self-Compassion Break *173*
   Forgiving Yourself..*173*
   Mindfulness Meditation *175*
   Develop a Self-Compassion Statement....................................*175*
   Resilience Through Self-Compassion *175*
   Celebrate Your Efforts *176*
   Reflective Journaling *176*
   Visualization: Seeing Yourself With Compassion......................*177*
PERSONAL REFLECTION FOR EMBRACING YOUR TRUE SELF *178*
   How Values Shape Authenticity..*179*
   A Call to Reflection *179*
EXERCISE: PERSONAL REFLECTION FOR EMBRACING YOUR TRUE SELF............................*180*
   Identifying Your Core Values *180*
   Understanding How Values Inform Authenticity.......................*181*
   Reflective Questions for Deep Introspection *182*
   Unearthing Hidden Fears and Desires *184*
   Recognizing Growth Opportunities *185*
   Create an Action Plan..*185*
   Regular Check-Ins *186*
EXPLORING AUTHENTICITY: DEFINING YOUR TRUE SELF *186*
   Authenticity Starts With Self-Acceptance.................................*187*
   Breaking Free From Barriers..*187*
   The Role of Accountability Partners *188*

CHAPTER 10: CREATING LASTING CHANGE **190**

SETTING UP DAILY SELF-CARE PRACTICES *191*
   Morning Rituals: Starting Your Day With Purpose *191*
   Evening Wind-Down: Finding Peace at Day's End....................*191*
   Weekly Self-Care Check-Ins: Staying on Track *193*
EXERCISE: CREATING A SELF-CARE TOOL KIT *194*
   Understanding the Importance of a Self-Care Tool Kit..............*194*

- *Gather Your Tool Kit Essentials*...195
- *Identifying Activities and Resources*......................................195
- *Evaluating Your Resources*..196
- *Building Your Tool Kit*..197
- *Incorporate Variety*...198
- *Regularly Update Your Tool Kit*...198
- *Using Your Self-Care Tool Kit*..198
- UNDERSTANDING THE IMPORTANCE OF EMOTIONAL RESILIENCE 198
  - *Benefits of Building Resilience*..199
  - *Building Resilience: Practical Strategies*.............................199
  - *Revisiting Resilience When Needed*....................................200
- EXERCISES FOR INTEGRATING SELF-CARE INTO EVERYDAY LIFE 200
  - *Mindfulness Moments: Little Breathers, Big Impact*............202
  - *Five-Minute Daily Gratitude: A Boost for Your Mood*..........202
  - *Self-Care Commitments: A Promise to Yourself*.................203
  - *Creating Community Support: Self-Care Together*.............203

CONCLUSION 205

RESOURCES FOR CONTINUED GROWTH 209

- *Support Groups and Communities*...209
- *Mental Health Resources*..210

REFERENCES..211

Introduction

When was the last time you felt like you were enough? If it's been a while, I know how that feels because I've been there myself. You see, this isn't just a workbook—it's a safe haven, a road map crafted with empathy and understanding from someone who's walked miles in shoes similar to yours. It's about time we rewrite the scripts of negativity that sometimes play all too loudly in our minds.

Let me take you through my story. I grew up in an environment where abuse wasn't just frequent; it was the norm. My parents often told me they didn't want me—it was something that echoed throughout my childhood. Those experiences left scars deep within my heart. And if that wasn't enough, life threw another curveball my way. Just when I thought I'd found some measure of stability, my husband left me for my best friend while I was three months pregnant. Betrayal stacked on top of rejection. I questioned my worth, believing maybe my parents were right after all. Maybe, just maybe, I really was as undesirable as I'd been made to feel.

But I refused to let those painful narratives define who I am. Instead, I began to understand my own power. I realized I was more than just the sum total of others' harsh words and actions. I decided to embark on a journey to reshape how I saw myself, and now, I'm proud to say that I'm ready to share what I've learned with you.

This workbook is your personal guide to changing negative self-talk into empowering affirmations, your confidante in the wee hours when doubt creeps in unnoticed. It follows the principles of my previous book, *Break Free From Negative Thinking: A Woman's Guide to Transforming Self-Talk, Managing Stress, and Building Lasting Confidence and Self-Love*, but dives deeper into practical exercises aimed at personal transformation. Consider it your trusted friend on this voyage to truth and freedom. Through this guide, we'll work together to smash the barriers that keep us shackled to false beliefs and step confidently into a space filled with self-love and resilience.

Throughout your time here, I want you to feel like we're sitting across from each other, two friends sharing a warm cup of coffee, words flowing naturally between us. This is the energy I want to cultivate with you: a conversational, no-judgment safe zone where you can explore the intricacies of your thoughts. I want you to think of this book as a cozy chat between friends—it's informal, relaxed, and designed to make you feel supported every step of the way.

You'll find, as you dive into these pages, that they're packed with strategies to help you recognize and challenge the negative tapes playing in your head. I'll introduce you to tools to change that inner dialogue so you can see yourself in a new, empowering light. We're also going to talk about resilience—how to build it and let it guide you through life's inevitable ups and downs with grace.

Now, here comes the fun part: This workbook isn't about rigid rules or fixed timelines. It's about *you*. You're encouraged to approach it at your own pace. If a certain exercise feels like too much today, that's perfectly okay. Allow yourself the flexibility to skip around. Savor the freedom to come back to parts whenever you feel ready. This is your journey, tailored by you, for you.

One of the key elements in making meaningful change is reflection. It's a powerful tool. As you work through the exercises, take time to write down your thoughts. Journaling is such a transformative practice because it lets you track where you've been and where you'd like to go. You don't have to wait for big moments either—sometimes the quiet revelations are the ones that change us the most. Revisit your reflections often, and be gentle with yourself. Celebrate your progress, even if it's just an inch forward, and never underestimate the beauty of small steps.

Throughout this workbook, you'll encounter exercises designed not just to challenge you but to nurture you, to encourage mindfulness and vulnerability in daily life. Here, vulnerability isn't a weakness; it's a superpower. It opens doors to authentic connections with yourself and others.

I know from my own experience that empowerment doesn't simply appear overnight. It requires patience, compassion, and a willingness to push past comfort zones. But here's what I promise: You're not alone. I'm right here with you, rooting for you during every struggle and every win. We've got an incredible adventure ahead of us, and I'm excited to see you unfold into the radiant person you already are beneath the layers of doubt.

So, take a deep breath and dive in. Trust in the process and, most importantly, trust in yourself. Remember, life isn't about being perfect; it's about being whole. Let's reclaim your narrative and begin a dialogue where self-doubt is changed into confidence and self-love. You are enough, and together, we'll walk this path to growing into the fullness of who you truly are.

Chapter 1:

Understanding the Roots of Negative Self-Talk

Let's get real for a second—how often do you find yourself saying things to yourself that you'd *never* say to someone you care about? That inner voice can be downright brutal, can't it? It's like carrying around a little critic on your shoulder, whispering doubts and pointing out every little flaw. It's important to understand that voice didn't just appear out of nowhere. It's a reflection of the experiences, messages, and beliefs you've picked up along the way.

In this chapter, we're going to unravel the mystery of where that negative self-talk comes from. We'll dig into its roots—those little moments and patterns that taught you to second-guess yourself. More importantly, I'll share practical exercises to turn the volume down on that critical voice and replace it with one that's kind, supportive, and, dare I say, empowering.

Because you are enough, exactly as you are. Let's start learning how to believe that for real.

Identify Personal Triggers and Their Origins

Let's pause for a moment and think about the last time you caught yourself spiraling into negative self-talk. Was it after a stressful meeting? Maybe it was while scrolling through social media, comparing yourself to that friend who always seems to have it all together. Or perhaps it was something smaller—like spilling coffee on your shirt and calling yourself "so clumsy." Whatever it was, that moment holds a clue, a little breadcrumb leading to the root of your inner critic.

Negative self-talk doesn't pop out of thin air. It's often sparked by triggers—those environmental or emotional stimuli that flip the switch on self-doubt. Triggers can be external, like criticism from others or seeing someone else's success. They can also be internal, such as feeling overwhelmed or tired. Recognizing these triggers is like shining a flashlight in a dark room—it's the first step in reclaiming control over your thoughts. When you know what's setting off that inner critic, you can start to shift your response.

Now, let's take it deeper. Where do those reactions come from? Often, they're rooted in your past. Maybe a critical teacher, a parent's high expectations, or a string of tough experiences taught you to see yourself in a certain way. Reflecting on your history isn't about blame; it's about understanding. When you uncover those patterns, you realize, *Oh, that's why I think like this*—and you begin to loosen their grip on your present.

Finally, let's get specific. Think about the situations where your inner critic tends to show up loud and clear. Is it when you're trying something new? When you're around certain people? Pinpointing these moments doesn't just help you become more self-aware; it also allows you to prepare. If you know that walking into a room full of strangers makes your self-doubt flare, you can equip yourself with tools to manage it.

Remember: Awareness is power, and you've already got what it takes to start rewriting the story.

Exercise: Identifying Specific Situations of Negative Self-Talk

Reflect and Write

- Take a moment in a quiet space to think about the times negative self-talk arises in your life.

- Write down specific situations where you notice this negative thinking. Consider contexts like work, relationships, social gatherings, or personal challenges.

_____
_____
_____
_____
_____
_____
_____
_____
_____
_____
_____
_____
_____
_____
_____
_____

Set the Scene

For each situation identified, describe the context. Ask yourself:

- Where were you?

_____
_____
_____
_____

- Who were you with?

_____
_____
_____
_____

- What were you doing at the time?

_____
_____
_____
_____

Notice Your Thoughts

After outlining the situation, write down the exact negative thoughts that ran through your mind. Be honest and specific.

_____
_____
_____
_____
_____

Identify Triggers

Look for patterns in these situations:

- What common threads do you see?

_____
_____
_____
_____
_____

- Do certain people, places, or events trigger negative thoughts?

_____
_____
_____

_____
_____

Coping Strategies

For each situation, brainstorm one or two coping strategies that could help counteract the negative self-talk. This could be affirmations, breathing exercises, or seeking support from others.

_____
_____
_____
_____
_____
_____
_____
_____

Regular Check-Ins

Commit to regularly reviewing your list of situations and reflections. This will enhance your self-awareness and help reinforce the positive changes you want to make.

When you follow this exercise, you'll actively engage in recognizing when and why negative self-talk appears, empowering you to develop strategies for breaking free from its hold.

Journal Exercise to Uncover Trigger Patterns

If you've ever thought, *Why does this always happen to me?*—or *Why do I keep reacting this way?*—then journaling is about to become your new best friend. Writing things down has a magical way of making the swirling chaos in your head feel tangible and, most importantly, manageable. Through this exercise, you'll uncover the roots of your triggers, explore the patterns behind your negative self-talk, and equip you to break free from the cycle.

Daily Journaling

Start with a simple habit: Carve out a few minutes each day to jot down your thoughts. Focus specifically on your self-talk—when it happens, what triggered it, and how it made you feel. Over time, these daily reflections will reveal recurring themes in your inner dialogue. Maybe you notice that your inner critic gets louder on days when you're stressed or when you spend too much time comparing yourself to others. Journaling creates a safe, nonjudgmental space to explore these feelings and begin making connections.

Trigger Tracking Grid

To take it up a notch, try creating a trigger tracking grid. This structured approach turns your reflections into data, helping you analyze patterns systematically. Plus, having a visual aid makes it easier to spot trends. For example, you might realize that criticism from authority figures consistently leaves you feeling not good enough. Now you know exactly what to work on.

Let's look at an example of how a trigger tracking grid might look. Feel free to customize it to suit your needs, but this format provides a clear structure to identify and analyze your triggers.

Date	Trigger	Negative thoughts	Emotions felt	Physical reactions	Possible alternative thoughts
Jan 2, 2025	Boss criticized my work	*I'm terrible at my job.*	Embarrassed, anxious	Tight chest, sweating	*This feedback helps me grow.*
Jan 3, 2025	Saw a friend's vacation pics	*My life isn't exciting enough.*	Jealous, unworthy	Clenched jaw, low energy	*I can plan a fun trip when it works for me.*
Jan 4, 2025	Forgot to respond to an email	*I'm so disorganized and lazy.*	Guilty, frustrated	Restlessness, headache	*I'm human; I'll reply and move on.*
Jan 5, 2025	Argument with a sibling	*They always think I'm wrong.*	Hurt, defensive	Racing heart, shaky hands	*I can calmly explain my perspective.*

How to Use the Grid

When you use this grid consistently, you'll begin to notice patterns and develop more empowering responses to situations that typically trigger negative self-talk.

- **Trigger:** Write down the event, situation, or interaction that triggered your negative self-talk.

- **Negative thoughts:** Capture the exact thoughts that came to mind.

- **Emotions felt:** Identify the emotions you experienced in response.

- **Physical reactions:** Note any physical sensations, such as a racing heart, muscle tension, or shallow breathing.

- **Possible alternative thoughts:** Reframe the negative thought into something more constructive or self-compassionate.

Prompting Reflection

If staring at a blank page feels overwhelming, use prompts to guide your journaling. Here are a few to get you started:

- What situation triggered negative self-talk today?

_____

_____

_____

- What thoughts went through my mind in that moment?

- How did I feel emotionally and physically?

_____
_____
_____
_____
_____

- Have I experienced a similar trigger before? What happened then?

_____
_____
_____
_____
_____

- What could I tell myself instead to shift my perspective next time?

_____
_____
_____
_____
_____

These prompts encourage deeper exploration and help you uncover the layers beneath your initial reactions, leading to greater self-awareness.

Monthly Review

At the end of each month, set aside time to review your journal entries. Look for common triggers, repeated thought patterns, or changes in how you're responding. This reflection is where the magic happens. It not only solidifies your understanding but also highlights your progress. Maybe you notice you're catching negative self-talk faster or handling certain triggers with more grace. Celebrate those wins—they're proof of your growth.

Develop a Plan to Track and Manage Triggers

Recognizing your triggers is a powerful step, but what comes next is equally important: creating a plan to manage them. Think of this as your personal road map to reclaiming control over your thoughts, one step at a time. When you track and proactively manage your triggers, you'll be equipped to handle tough moments with confidence and resilience.

A solid plan is like having a tool kit for your mind. Start by outlining strategies to handle the triggers you've identified. For example:

- If a specific situation consistently sparks negative self-talk, like receiving criticism, decide in advance how you'll respond. Maybe it's taking three deep breaths, reminding yourself it's not personal, and reframing the feedback as constructive.

- For environmental triggers, like social media, set boundaries. Limit screen time or unfollow accounts that feed negativity.

Tailoring the plan to your needs empowers you to stay proactive, integrating self-compassion and mindfulness into your daily life. It's your commitment to personal growth in action.

Setting Realistic Goals

Your plan will work best when it's grounded in achievable steps. Instead of aiming to completely eliminate negative self-talk overnight, set smaller, realistic goals. For instance:

- "I'll journal my triggers and responses three times this week."
- "I'll use one positive affirmation daily when I catch myself being self-critical."

These specific, actionable goals provide a clear path forward. Be mindful of celebrating your wins! Each step, no matter how small, is progress.

That moment when you notice a trigger and respond differently? That's worth acknowledging—and it builds momentum for lasting change.

And remember, you don't have to go it alone. Enlist the help of trusted friends, family members, or professionals to support your journey:

- Share your plan with a close friend or family member and ask them to check in with you.

- Join a support group or community where others are working on similar goals.

- Consider working with a therapist or coach who can guide you through challenging moments.

Having a support system not only provides accountability but also reminds you that you're not alone. Leaning on others builds resilience and opens you to new perspectives and strategies.

Reflection and Revision

Plans aren't static—they're living, breathing guides. Take time weekly or monthly to decide on what's working for you and what simply isn't. Ask yourself:

- Are there new triggers I've noticed?

_____

_____

_____

- Is there a strategy I've been avoiding that I could reintroduce?

- What progress have I made, and how can I build on it?

Developing a plan to track and manage triggers is about taking ownership of your journey. It's your chance to create a system that works for you, one that supports your growth and reminds you of your strength. And remember—every step forward, no matter how small, is a step closer to becoming the person you're striving to be.

By now, you've uncovered the roots of your negative self-talk, mapped out your triggers, and started creating a plan to manage them. That's no small feat! You're building awareness, resilience, and a tool kit to handle those tough moments—and that's powerful.

But we're not stopping here. In the next chapter, we'll dive even deeper into the heart of the matter: your inner critic. You know, that voice that nitpicks and whispers doubts when you least need it. It's time to learn how to identify this sneaky saboteur and—here's the exciting part—challenge it. You have the power to rewrite the script in your mind, and I'll show you how to start.

Let's turn the page and give that inner critic a run for its money. You're ready for this!

Chapter 2:

How to Identify and Challenge Your Inner Critic

If your inner critic had a personality, it would probably be the most annoying person at the party. You know, the one whispering, "Everyone's judging you. You're not good enough." Sound familiar? This nagging voice thrives on keeping you small, second-guessing yourself, and assuming the worst. But that voice isn't the real you.

In this chapter, you'll discover practical ways to reframe negative thoughts, set boundaries with self-doubt, and build a mental toolbox that empowers you to feel more confident and at peace. By the end, you'll be ready to tell your inner critic, "Thanks for your input, but I've got this." Because you do.

Strategy for Acknowledging and Dialoguing With Your Inner Critic

Your inner critic isn't the villain of your story—it's more like a misguided friend who thinks they're helping but keeps getting it wrong. This part of you often speaks from a place shaped by past experiences, societal expectations, or the need to protect you from perceived failures. But instead of letting it run the show, you can learn to acknowledge its presence and engage in a healthier, more constructive dialogue.

Understanding Your Inner Critic

First, let's demystify this voice. Your inner critic isn't inherently bad—it's just loud and a little misguided. It usually stems from past experiences, like critical comments you internalized as a child or societal pressure to meet impossible standards. Recognizing this can help you see that it's not *your* truth—it's a reflection of things you've picked up along the way.

By naming and noticing when your inner critic shows up, you're already taking the first step toward changing negative self-talk. Acknowledging its presence can reduce its power over your emotions. Think of it this way: What we resist persists, but what we name, we tame.

Engaging in Constructive Dialogue

Once you've acknowledged your inner critic, the next step is to engage with it—yes, actually talk to it. Who says we can't still have imaginary friends, right? As an adult, this one can be a concerned yet overly dramatic one. Instead of shutting it down or trying to ignore it, ask it questions like:

- "What are you really worried about?"

_____
_____
_____
_____
_____

- "Why do you think this matters so much?"

_____
_____
_____

You might find that its intentions, though flawed, are rooted in fear or outdated beliefs. Respond with curiosity rather than judgment.

When you speak to your inner critic, use a compassionate tone. For example, instead of snapping back with "You're wrong!", try saying, "I understand you're trying to protect me, but I don't need that right now." This approach shifts the dynamic, making space for self-awareness and growth.

Finally, set boundaries. You can thank your inner critic for its input while firmly asserting your worth. For instance, say something like: "I appreciate the concern, but I'm capable and enough as I am. I choose to focus on what I can do, not on what you think I lack."

When you acknowledge and dialogue with your inner critic, you reclaim the narrative. You're no longer passively accepting its commentary but actively shaping the way you see yourself. This practice creates self-awareness, builds emotional resilience, and reminds you that you're worthy of your own support and compassion. After all, who better to stand up for you than *you*?

Exercise: Engaging in Constructive Dialogue With Your Inner Critic

When exploring this exercise, you'll strengthen your ability to interact with your inner critic positively, promoting understanding, compassion, and growth in your journey to break free from negative thinking.

Set the Scene

Find a comfortable and quiet space where you can relax without interruptions.

Identify Your Inner Critic

Take a moment to acknowledge your inner critic:

- What does it sound like?

_____
_____
_____
_____
_____

- How does it express itself?

_____
_____
_____
_____
_____

- Write down a few common phrases or thoughts that this voice typically uses.

_____
_____
_____

Initiate a Dialogue

Imagine you're having a conversation with your inner critic. Start by addressing it directly. For example, "I hear you trying to protect me, but I'd like to understand more."

Ask Questions

Use open-ended questions to explore the motivations behind your inner critic's voice. Consider asking:

- What are you trying to achieve by saying this?

- What fear are you trying to protect me from?

_____
_____
_____
_____
_____

- How does this thought serve me right now?

_____
_____
_____
_____
_____

Practice Compassion

As you engage with your inner critic, respond with a compassionate tone. Acknowledge its intentions, even if you disagree. For instance, you could say, "I appreciate your concern, but I need to remind you that I'm capable and worthy."

Establish Boundaries

Clearly assert your worth in this conversation. You might say something like, "I recognize that I may not be perfect, but I'm enough as I am." This sets a boundary with your inner critic while maintaining a respectful dialogue.

Reflect on the Conversation

After the dialogue, take a moment to reflect on what you learned. Write down any insights or shifts in perspective that occurred during the exercise.

_____

_____

_____

Regular Practice

Make this dialogue a regular practice. The more you engage with your inner critic constructively, the easier it will become to create a more balanced and compassionate self-talk.

Reframing Your Inner Dialogue

Once you've created mental space, you can begin changing how you engage with your inner critic. Instead of letting it dictate your narrative, use these techniques to reclaim the conversation.

Anchor Phrases or Mantras

Sometimes, all it takes is a powerful phrase to counteract negativity. Write down a mantra that rings true with you, such as:

- "I am enough."
- "I deserve kindness—from others and from myself."

When your inner critic pipes up, repeat your mantra like a grounding truth. These phrases can anchor you in moments of doubt and remind you of your worth.

Rescripting Your Inner Narrative

Rewrite the story your inner critic is telling. For instance, if it says, "You'll never get this right," respond with, "I'm learning, and that's enough for now." Shift the narrative from defeat to growth, reminding yourself that progress, not perfection, is the goal.

Self-Compassion as a Superpower

The most transformative tool in reframing your dialogue is self-compassion. Speak to yourself the way you'd comfort a close friend. Replace harsh judgments with soothing, affirming words, like: "I understand why I feel this way, and it's okay. I'm doing my best, and that's all that matters." This approach softens your inner critic's harsh edges, fostering a sense of safety and self-worth.

When you create space for reflection and reframe your inner dialogue, you shift from being at the mercy of your inner critic to holding a seat of self-empowerment. These practices not only quiet the critical voice but change it into a springboard for growth, resilience, and deeper self-love. Because when you make space for yourself, you'll find that you're far more than enough.

Exercise: Reframing Your Inner Dialogue for Empowerment

When you engage in this exercise, you'll create a more empowering internal conversation, allowing you to break free from negative thinking and welcome the transformative power of self-compassion.

Identify Negative Phrases

Begin by taking a moment to jot down negative thoughts or phrases you often tell yourself. These might include statements like "I'm not good enough" or "I always mess things up."

_____
_____
_____
_____

Transform the Dialogue

For each negative phrase, practice reframing it into a more empowering statement. For example, change "I can't handle this" to "I am capable of finding solutions."

_____
_____

Create Anchor Phrases

Develop a list of anchor phrases or mantras that resonate with you. These should be short, positive affirmations that you can easily recall during moments of self-doubt. Examples include:

- "I am worthy of love and respect."
- "Every obstacle is a chance for growth."
- "I embrace my imperfections; they make me unique."

Practice Rescripting

Select one of your negative thoughts and write a short paragraph rescripting your inner narrative. Focus on the positive aspects of the situation, what you learned, and how you can move forward. For instance, if your original thought was, *I failed*, rescript it to, "I took a valuable lesson from this experience that will help me in the future."

_____
_____
_____
_____
_____
_____

Emphasize Self-Compassion

As you practice rescripting, remind yourself to approach this exercise with self-compassion. If you catch yourself slipping back into negative thinking, gently redirect with kindness. You might say, "It's okay to feel this way; I'm doing my best, and I deserve grace."

_____
_____
_____

_____

_____

Repeat and Reinforce

Make a habit of reciting your anchor phrases daily, especially when you notice negative self-talk creeping in. You could say them in front of a mirror or jot them down in your journal to reinforce their power.

Reflect on the Impact

After a week of practicing this exercise, take time to reflect on any changes in your mindset. Write about how reframing your inner dialogue has affected your thoughts, feelings, and actions.

_____

_____

_____

_____

_____

_____

_____

_____

Personification of Your Inner Critic

Your inner critic doesn't have to remain an invisible, overpowering force in your mind. By turning it into a character—a persona—you can step back, see it more clearly, and challenge it effectively.

Imagine your inner critic as someone you'd meet in a story: a bossy coworker, an overbearing relative, or perhaps a grumpy troll under a bridge. Giving it a name, a personality, and even a physical appearance helps you externalize it, which can greatly reduce its emotional hold over you. Maybe your inner critic has a sharp, impatient voice, or perhaps it's quiet but insistent. Picture its demeanor—does it wag a finger, roll its eyes, or sigh dramatically? Adding humor or exaggeration, like dressing it in mismatched socks or giving it an oversized hat, can make the exercise fun and empowering. By making the critic tangible, you can better recognize its biases and exaggerations, often realizing how irrational or outdated its messages are.

Dialogue With the Persona

Once you've created this persona, it's time to start a conversation. Think of it as a role-play where you call the shots. Begin by asking questions. Often, the critic's reasoning is based on flawed assumptions or unspoken fears. Writing these conversations helps you practice calm, confident replies and even allows you to highlight the absurdity of some critical thoughts. If your inner critic says, "You'll never be good enough," you can respond with, "Good enough for what? According to who?" This exercise not only exposes the critic's weak points but also equips you to handle real-life moments of self-doubt more constructively.

Evaluating the Persona's Arguments

Your inner critic loves to speak in absolutes, but its claims often crumble under scrutiny. Start by questioning its statements. These questions help you separate fact from fiction. You can also validate your personal experiences to directly challenge its suggestions. If your critic tells you, "You'll fail because you always do," remind yourself of the many times you've succeeded. Dig deeper to understand the critic's motivations—often, its negativity comes from a place of fear or a misplaced sense of protection. Recognizing this can shift your perspective, allowing you to respond with compassion instead of frustration.

Changing the Character

The ultimate goal isn't to silence your inner critic but to change it into a more supportive figure. Look for its positive traits or intentions, like its attempts to protect you from harm or failure. Acknowledge these, but guide the critic to adopt a kinder tone. You might even imagine creating a supportive counterpart—a cheerleader, mentor, or wise friend—to balance the dialogue in your mind. Over time, you can encourage your inner critic to shift from a harsh naysayer to a thoughtful advisor. Instead of hearing, "You'll never succeed," you might eventually hear, "Let's think this through so you're ready to succeed."

When you personify your inner critic, you take control of the narrative. This practice allows you to externalize, engage with, and ultimately change this critical voice into one that empowers and supports you.

Exercise: Personification of Your Inner Critic

This exercise allows you to create a clearer understanding of your inner critic, empowering you to confront it with creativity and compassion and, ultimately, to break free from negative thinking.

Creating a Critic Persona

- Start by envisioning your inner critic as a character. In the space provided, sketch or describe this persona. Consider their appearance, voice, and demeanor. What kind of clothes do they wear? Do they have a specific tone or mannerisms?

- Give your inner critic a name that resonates with you. This helps create a tangible representation, making it easier to challenge and confront.

Visualizing the Critic

- Spend a few moments visualizing your critic persona in specific situations where their voice is prominent. Note the exaggerations and biases in their messaging. Write down examples of how they might misinterpret situations or amplify your fears.

Dialogue With the Persona

- Now, conduct a scripted dialogue with this character. Write out a conversation between you and your critic. Start with a prompt like, "Why do you think I can't succeed?" Allow your critic to respond.

- After each response, write your counterpoint. Challenge their assertions—this role-playing can highlight the absurdity of certain critical thoughts. Practice different responses to prepare for real-world moments of self-doubt.

_____
_____

Evaluate the Persona's Arguments

- Go through the responses in your dialogue and critically assess the arguments made by your inner critic. Ask yourself:

    o Are these statements truly accurate, or are they overstated?

_____
_____
_____
_____
_____

- What personal experiences contradict these claims?

___

- What might be the motivations behind these negative comments?

___

- Write down your findings, emphasizing your strengths and successes that counter the critic's claims.

___

Transforming the Character

- Think about how you can evolve your inner critic into a more supportive figure. Identify any positive traits or intentions your critic might have. For example, if they want to protect you from failure, acknowledge that intention.

_____
_____
_____
_____
_____

- Develop a supportive counterpart to this persona. Sketch or describe this character, focusing on their encouraging qualities. What do they say to uplift you during times of doubt?

_____
_____
_____

- Write a final dialogue where your supportive persona counsels you, emphasizing growth, acceptance, and self-love.

_____

_____

Reflection and Integration

- After completing the dialogue and transformation, take a moment to reflect on the experience. How has visualizing your inner critic changed your perspective? Write about how this exercise might help in challenging negative thoughts in real life.

_____
_____
_____
_____
_____
_____
_____
_____

Technique for Transforming Critical Thoughts

Critical thoughts often sneak in unnoticed, shaping how we see ourselves and the world. But with intentional effort, you can replace these unhelpful narratives with affirmations and more supportive self-talk. This technique focuses on recognizing and reframing these thoughts, turning a habitual critic into a source of encouragement.

Recognizing Automatic Negative Thoughts

The first step in changing critical thoughts is awareness. Automatic negative thoughts, or ANTs, are those reflexive, unhelpful comments that pop into your mind without invitation. They often sound like, "You're not worthy," or "You'll never succeed." By becoming conscious of these thoughts, you gain the power to challenge them.

Awareness doesn't mean overanalyzing every thought. Instead, it's about pausing when a negative thought arises and noting its presence.

Understanding the triggers behind ANTs is another crucial step. Are these thoughts more frequent in certain situations, like before a big presentation or after receiving constructive feedback? Identifying triggers prepares your mind to respond proactively, reducing the likelihood of falling into old patterns.

Recognizing recurring patterns also helps establish a foundation for change. Perhaps you notice a tendency to catastrophize—immediately jumping to worst-case scenarios—or to overgeneralize by thinking, *I always mess things up*. These patterns often stem from past experiences but don't need to define your present. Once you recognize them, you can challenge their validity.

Reframing and Replacing Negative Thoughts

Awareness is only the first step; the real change happens when you consciously replace critical thoughts with positive, affirming ones. Start by questioning the truth of an ANT. If you think, *I can't handle this,* ask yourself, "Is that really true? What evidence do I have that I've handled difficult situations before?"

After challenging the thought, create a replacement that's both realistic and empowering. Instead of *I'll fail,* try *I'm learning, and every step I take gets me closer to my goal.* This isn't about ignoring challenges but reframing them in a way that acknowledges your resilience and capability.

Using affirmations as a tool for replacement can be incredibly effective. Choose phrases that resonate with you, such as:

- "I am capable and resourceful."
- "I can grow from challenges."

Repeat these affirmations consistently, especially when negative thoughts arise, to reinforce a new mental narrative.

This practice fosters self-compassion and encourages growth, replacing criticism with constructive and affirming perspectives.

Exercise: Transforming Critical Thoughts Into Positive Affirmations

When you work through this exercise, you'll create a greater awareness of your ANTs while laying the groundwork for changing them into positive self-talk, empowering you to break free from the constraints of negativity.

Recognizing ANTs

- Begin by keeping a journal for a week, noting down instances when you experience negative self-talk. Pay attention to specific phrases or thoughts that pop up frequently. This could include something like *I'm always messing up* or *I don't deserve love.*

- Each time you notice an ANT, write it down. This helps create awareness of these negative narratives and paves the way for change.

Understanding Triggers

- As you reflect on your journal entries, identify and note any triggers that lead to these ANTs. Are there specific situations, people, or stressors that provoke negative thoughts? Understanding these triggers can help you prepare your mind for a more constructive response in the future.

_____
_____
_____
_____
_____
_____
_____
_____
_____
_____

Recognizing Patterns

- Look for patterns in your ANTs. Are there recurring themes? Do they typically arise in certain contexts, such as during work presentations or social gatherings? Recognizing these patterns establishes a foundation for understanding where you need to focus your efforts.

_____
_____
_____
_____
_____

Crafting Positive Affirmations

- For every ANT you documented, create a positive affirmation that counters it. Transform your negative statements into empowering ones. For example:

    o Change "I can't do anything right" to "I learn and grow from every experience."

    o Shift "I'm not worthy of love" to "I am deserving of love and respect."

_____
_____
_____
_____
_____

Daily Affirmation Practice

- Choose a few of your newly composed affirmations to focus on daily. Write them on sticky notes and place them where you can see them—on your mirror, computer, or refrigerator.

- Every morning, take a few moments to read these affirmations aloud. Feel their truth as you speak them, allowing the positive energy to resonate with you.

Response Preparation

- When you sense an ANT emerging, pause and remind yourself of the affirmation you constructed. Practice acknowledging the critical thought without judgment and consciously replacing it with your positive statement. This shifts your mindset and prepares you for real-life moments of self-doubt.

Reflection

- At the end of the week, take some time to reflect on the impact of this exercise. Write about any shifts you noticed in your mindset or emotional responses. How did replacing negative thoughts with affirmations affect your daily life?

_____

_____

_____

_____

_____

_____

_____

_____

You've just tackled one of the hardest challenges: facing your inner critic head-on. You've learned to recognize its voice, name it, and even sit down for a chat without letting it take over the conversation. You've also explored ways to create mental space, challenge those ANTs, and change criticism into kindness. Step by step, you're reclaiming your inner dialogue, and that's a win!

Get ready for the next chapter, because we're diving into rewriting your inner narrative. If your inner critic has been the director of your mental movie for too long, it's time to take the pen back. We'll explore how to craft a story that reflects your strength, growth, and boundless potential. Because you're so much more than the voice of doubt in your head—you're the author of your own story, and it's about to get really, really good.

Let's turn the page and keep building the narrative you truly deserve. Onward!

Chapter 3:

Rewriting Your Inner Narrative

Imagine for a moment that your inner voice isn't a bully; it's your best friend. Sounds impossible, right? I get it. When self-doubt and negative self-talk have been running the show for so long, it's easy to believe that's just how things are. But honestly, you can change the story you tell yourself. And when you do, everything else begins to change too.

This chapter is all about taking the pen back from that overly critical narrator in your head. It's time to explore practical, empowering techniques to rewrite the narrative that plays on repeat. You'll learn how to recognize the lies self-doubt feeds you, challenge them, and replace them with truths that remind you just how capable, worthy, and enough you are.

Crafting Unique Positive Affirmations

Let's be honest, repeating "I'm a millionaire" isn't going to magically fill your bank account (if only it worked that way, right?). But affirmations do have real power when they're personal, meaningful, and grounded in your reality. Think of them as tiny seeds you plant in your mind that, when nurtured with consistency and care, grow into a more confident and self-assured you.

At their core, affirmations are short, powerful statements that challenge the negative chatter in your head and replace it with something constructive. And science backs this up—affirmations can rewire your brain by creating new neural pathways for positive thinking (Cascio et al., 2016). They act like a counterweight to self-doubt, tipping the scale back toward self-belief.

The best part? Affirmations don't have to be generic or cheesy. When they resonate with your own experiences and goals, they become your inner encourager. Imagine swapping out "I'm a failure" for "I'm capable of learning and growing." That simple shift? It's like flipping on a light in a dark room.

Affirmation Practice

The secret to making affirmations work is blending them into your daily life. Think of them as little mental check-ins. Start your day by saying them while brushing your teeth, or jot them down in your journal at night. Choose moments when you're relaxed and focused—like during your morning coffee or before bed—so they really sink in.

If you want to take it a step further, share your affirmations with a good friend. Not only does this create accountability, but it also builds a support system where you cheer each other on. Plus, there's something beautifully validating about hearing someone else affirm what you're working toward.

Making Them Yours

Here's your challenge: Think up affirmations that sound like you. Forget generic phrases and focus on what you truly need to hear. For example, if you're working on self-worth, try something like, "I deserve love and respect, starting with myself." If confidence is your goal, how about, "I am enough, exactly as I am, and I'm growing every day."

The real change happens when your affirmations speak directly to your heart. They'll feel less like empty words and more like a promise you're keeping to yourself. And when you repeat them regularly, you're training your brain to believe in that promise.

So, grab a pen, dig deep, and devise affirmations that empower you. Because the story you're writing? It's one where you show up as your strongest, most unapologetically confident self. Let's make it happen.

Exercise: Creating Personal Affirmations

Understand the Challenge

Begin by reflecting on any negative beliefs you currently hold about yourself. Write down these beliefs to identify the areas where you want to create change.

_____
_____
_____
_____
_____
_____
_____
_____

Reframe the Beliefs

For each negative belief, write a positive statement that counters it. Make sure these affirmations are in the present tense, focusing on what you want to embody now.

- Example:
    - Negative belief: "I'm not good enough."
    - Affirmation: "I am worthy and capable of greatness."

_____

_____

Personalize Your Affirmations

Tailor your affirmations to resonate with your individual experiences and desires. Use specific language that feels authentic to you:

- Consider including aspects such as your name, your goals, or personal values.

- Example: "I, [your name], embrace my unique talents and share them confidently with the world."

_____

_____

_____

_____
_____
_____
_____
_____

Experiment With Formulations

Try different words, phrases, and structures until you find formulations that resonate deeply with you. Play around with your affirmations to see what feels most powerful.

- For instance, you might change "I am brave" to "I courageously face challenges every day."

_____
_____
_____

Establish an Affirmation Practice

- Create a routine to incorporate your affirmations into your daily life. Consider these suggestions:

    - **Morning ritual:** Recite your affirmations each morning to set a positive tone for the day.

    - **Mindful moments:** Take a few moments during the day, especially when feeling doubt, to pause and repeat your affirmations.

    - **Evening reflection:** Close your day by reflecting on your affirmations and how you've embodied them throughout the day.

- **Choose the right moments:** Write down specific moments in your day when you can effectively practice your affirmations. This might be while commuting, during meditation, or before important events.

Share With Friends

Consider sharing your affirmations with supportive friends. This can create a sense of accountability and create a space for mutual encouragement.

This exercise allows you to create personal affirmations that challenge negative beliefs and reinforce a more positive, empowered mindset.

Evaluating Effectiveness

Affirmations aren't a "set it and forget it" kind of thing—they're more like a work in progress, and that's the beauty of it. To truly reap their benefits, it's important to pause and assess how they're working for you. But how you can evaluate their impact and keep your practice fresh and effective?

Start by keeping a simple journal or notes on your phone. Write down how you feel about yourself when you begin using affirmations, then revisit those notes weekly or monthly. Has your self-talk changed? Are you being kinder to yourself? Seeing these changes written down is like getting a high five from your past self.

Take a moment to compare your mindset before and after you started using affirmations. Do you feel more confident? Are you less quick to criticize yourself? Progress might be subtle, like feeling less anxious about speaking up in a meeting, but those little wins add up.

Affirmations are meant to grow with you, not hold you back. If one stops resonating or feels stale, don't hesitate to tweak it. Maybe "I'm learning to trust myself" evolves into "I'm confident in my decisions." Keeping them aligned with where you are in your journey ensures they stay relevant and powerful.

Evaluating the effectiveness of your affirmations isn't just about measuring progress—it's a reminder of how far you've come. Celebrate those shifts, no matter how small, and keep evolving your affirmations as you continue to grow.

Implementing Visualization Techniques

Let's talk about visualization—a practice that's like creating a mental highlight reel of your best moments before they even happen. It's not just daydreaming with extra steps; it's a powerful tool that helps align your mind with your aspirations, paving the way for a more positive and empowered narrative.

At its core, visualization is about imagining yourself achieving your goals or facing challenges with confidence and ease. This isn't just woo-woo thinking; there's solid psychology behind it. When you vividly picture success, your brain processes it almost as if it's already happened. This boosts motivation and focus, making your goals feel not just possible but inevitable (Rathor, 2023).

Keep in mind that visualization isn't just for achieving the big stuff—it also helps for managing anxiety. When you mentally rehearse a situation, like giving a presentation or having a tough conversation, you're essentially creating a mental road map that makes the real thing feel less overwhelming. You're training your brain to respond with confidence instead of panic.

Think of visualization as a mini workout for your imagination. When you picture yourself succeeding, also try to engage all your senses. What does your success look like? What do you hear? What do you feel? For example, if your goal is to speak up confidently in meetings, imagine the

59

room, the warmth of your voice, and the nods of approval. The more vivid your mental imagery, the more your brain believes in the possibility.

This practice also helps build emotional resilience. Visualizing yourself handling challenges gracefully prepares you to stay calm and collected when life gets messy. It's like rehearsing strength and adaptability so you can bring your A game when it matters most.

To make visualization part of your routine, pair it with another habit—like your morning coffee or bedtime wind-down. Take a few moments to close your eyes and vividly imagine your goals, focusing on the positive feelings they bring. And if you're dealing with specific challenges, mentally rehearse how you'll manage them with confidence.

Visualization is more than just creating a perfect fantasy; it's about reminding yourself that you're capable of growth, change, and resilience.

So, let your imagination run wild in the best way possible—your empowered narrative is waiting to unfold.

Exercise: Guided Visualization for Challenging Negative Beliefs

When you engage in this guided visualization exercise, you'll create a powerful belief in your abilities and challenge those negative beliefs that hold you back.

Find Your Space

Begin by choosing a quiet, comfortable space where you can sit or lie down without distractions. This could be a comfortable space in your home, a peaceful park, or anywhere that makes you feel safe and at ease.

Set an Intention

Close your eyes, if you're comfortable doing so, and take a few deep breaths. Set a clear intention for your visualization. What negative belief are you challenging, and what positive outcome do you wish to visualize?

- Example: "I want to visualize myself confidently presenting my ideas."

_____
_____
_____

_____

_____

Begin Your Visualization

Picture yourself in a situation where you're successfully achieving your desired outcome. Imagine every detail vividly.

- **Scene setting:** What does the environment look like? Are you in a bright meeting room, on a stage, or in a coffee shop with friends?

_____
_____
_____
_____
_____

- **Body language:** Visualize how you're carrying yourself. Are you standing tall, smiling, and engaging others with confidence?

_____
_____
_____
_____

Incorporate Sensory Details

Enhance the experience by incorporating sensory details. What do you see, hear, feel, and even smell in this visualization?

- **Sight:** Are there colorful decorations, supportive faces, or natural elements around you?

_____
_____
_____
_____

- **Sound:** Hear the applause, the supportive words from your friends, or the sound of your own voice speaking confidently.

_____
_____
_____

_____

_____

- **Touch:** Feel the warmth of the room, the smooth surface of the table you're leaning against, or the comfortable fabric of your clothing.

_____

_____

_____

_____

- **Smell:** Notice any pleasant aromas, like coffee brewing or fresh flowers nearby.

_____

_____

_____

_____

Embrace the Emotions

Allow yourself to feel the emotions associated with this successful outcome. What joy, pride, or excitement arises within you? Let these positive feelings wash over you and fill your being.

_____

_____

_____

Affirm Your Experience

As you visualize, incorporate affirmations that reinforce your belief in this positive outcome.

- Example: "I'm capable and confident. I deserve success."

_____
_____
_____
_____
_____

Regular Practice

Commit to practicing this visualization regularly. Set aside a few minutes each day, whether in the morning to set a positive tone or in the evening to reflect on your day.

Journal Your Thoughts

After each visualization session, take a moment to jot down your thoughts and feelings. How did the experience feel? Did any new insights come to you?

_____
_____
_____

_____

_____

_____

_____

_____

_____

_____

Creating Vision Boards

If you've ever caught yourself doodling your dream life or pinning aspirational quotes on Pinterest, you're already halfway to understanding the magic of a vision board. It's like creating a visual playlist of your goals—a tangible reminder of what you're striving for and who you're becoming.

Vision boards are more than just pretty collages; they're motivational powerhouses. When you display images, words, and symbols that represent your goals, you're giving yourself a daily visual nudge to stay focused and inspired. They serve as a constant reminder of what you're working toward, helping you tune out distractions and keep your eyes on the prize.

Even better, vision boards create a subtle sense of accountability. Seeing those images every day reminds you of your intentions, making it harder to brush them aside when life gets busy. Plus, they're fun to make—it's like crafting your own personal pep talk.

To keep the energy alive, make updating your vision board a regular practice. Goals evolve, and your vision board should reflect that. Whether you've achieved a milestone or your dreams have shifted, refreshing your board ensures it stays aligned with where you are and where you want to go.

Combine your vision board with your affirmations for a one–two punch of positivity. Spend a few moments each day looking at your vision board while repeating your affirmations. For instance, if your vision board includes an image of a happy, confident version of you, pair it with an affirmation like, "I'm growing into the best version of myself every day."

This dual approach strengthens the connection between your thoughts and feelings, reinforcing your belief in what's possible. It's like creating a feedback loop of motivation—your vision board inspires your affirmations, and your affirmations breathe life into your vision.

Your vision board is a living, breathing narrative of the amazing life you're building. With it, you're not just dreaming—you're actively creating the future you want.

Exercise: Incorporating Affirmations and Visualizations Into Your Daily Routine

Recognize the Importance of Consistency

Understand that incorporating affirmations and visualizations into your routine is key to challenging negative beliefs and fostering personal growth. Consistency builds discipline and deepens the impact of these practices.

Build a Daily Practice

Start by committing to a daily practice that feels manageable and sustainable. Let's look at some strategies to help you establish that routine:

- **Choose specific times:** Write down specific times during your day when you can dedicate a few minutes to your affirmations and visualizations. This could be when you first wake up, while you have a break at lunch, or before you go to bed. Setting these times creates a sense of discipline.

_____
_____
_____
_____
_____

- **Pair with existing habits:** Integrate your affirmations and visualization practices into existing habits. For example, if you enjoy a morning coffee, take a few moments while you sip to recite your affirmations or visualize your goals. Combining these practices with routines you already have helps make them a natural part of your life.

Start Small

Begin with small steps to allow for gradual adjustments. It's okay to start with just a few affirmations or a short visualization session each day. As you build confidence and feel comfortable, you can gradually increase the duration or number of affirmations.

- **Example:** Start with just five minutes of visualization focused on one affirmation. As it becomes a comfortable part of your routine, you can extend this to ten minutes or add additional affirmations.

Create a Supportive Environment

Surround yourself with positivity in your practice space. Whether it's a calm corner of your home, your favorite chair, or a peaceful outdoor setting, make sure it's a place where you feel relaxed and inspired. Write down some suggestions:

_____
_____
_____
_____
_____

Track Your Progress

Consider tracking your daily affirmations and visualization sessions. Reflect on how you felt before and after each practice, and note any changes in your mindset or feelings about yourself over time.

_____
_____
_____

_____
_____
_____
_____
_____
_____
_____

Stay Flexible

Life can be unpredictable, so it's important to stay flexible with your routine. If you miss a day or two, don't be hard on yourself. Simply acknowledge it and return to your practice as soon as you can.

Celebrate Your Wins

Acknowledge and celebrate the small victories along the way. Each time you engage in your affirmations or visualizations, you're taking a positive step toward challenging negative beliefs and reinforcing your self-worth.

When you incorporate these practices into your daily routine, you'll create a powerful habit that nurtures your growth, builds confidence, and challenges those limiting beliefs that no longer serve you.

Exercise: Tracking Your Progress in Emotional Growth

Start a Journaling Practice

Begin by keeping a dedicated journal for your affirmations and visualizations. These pages are meant to be a valuable resource for reflection and growth. Each day, take a few moments to jot down your experiences, focusing on how you felt before and after your practices.

- **Prompt ideas:** What affirmations did you focus on today? How did the visualization make you feel? Did you notice any changes in your mindset or emotions throughout the day? Writing these reflections will help you spot trends and shifts over time.

Identify Patterns and Trends

As you continue journaling, look back over your entries every week or month to identify patterns. Are there particular affirmations that resonate more deeply or specific visualizations that evoke stronger emotions? Recognizing these trends can provide insight into your emotional growth and help you tailor future practices.

Utilize App Technology

Consider using apps designed for tracking habits or journaling. Many apps allow you to log your daily affirmations and visualizations easily. Some even have features for setting reminders or tracking mood changes, making it convenient to stay consistent with your practices.

- **Suggested apps:** Look for apps that offer journaling, habit tracking, or even mindfulness features. This can add an engaging tech element to your journey. Consider Habitify, Way of Life, HabitNow, or Streaks (Guinness, 2024).

Celebrate Small Victories

Take time to acknowledge and celebrate your progress, no matter how small. Each time you practice affirmations or visualizations, recognize that you're taking positive steps toward change.

- **Celebration idea:** Create a "win jar" where you write down small victories related to your emotional growth. Whenever you have a moment to celebrate—a day you felt particularly confident, a successful presentation, or simply feeling good about yourself—write it down and place it in the jar. Over time, it will fill up with reminders of your progress.

Reflect on Your Growth

Regularly set aside time to reflect on your overall emotional growth. How have your beliefs about yourself changed? Do you feel more confident or resilient? Use your journal entries, patterns, and celebrations to fuel a deeper understanding of your journey.

_____
_____
_____
_____
_____
_____
_____
_____
_____
_____

Share Your Journey

If you feel comfortable, consider sharing your journaling reflections or victories with a trusted friend or support group. This adds an extra layer of accountability and can foster meaningful conversations around growth and self-acceptance.

When you track your progress through these various methods, you'll gain valuable insights into your emotional growth and reinforce the positive changes that come from affirmations and visualizations. Welcome this journey of self-discovery, and celebrate the change that unfolds!

You're no longer stuck in old stories; you're the author of a new one. One where you welcome your strengths, honor your growth, and step into the confidence that comes with aligning your thoughts, feelings, and actions.

In the next chapter, we'll dive even deeper into building unshakeable self-esteem. You'll discover how to turn self-doubt into self-trust, break free from the weight of others' opinions, and truly believe in your own worth. Because you're not just enough—you're extraordinary. Let's keep going!

Chapter 4:

Building Unshakeable Self-Esteem

Picture yourself scrolling through your day, crushing your to-do list, when *bam*! A random thought smacks you like an unexpected text from an ex: *Do I even deserve a better life?* Cue the self-doubt spiral. Suddenly, you're replaying every awkward interaction since middle school and assuming everyone around you secretly thinks you're a walking disaster. Well, my friend, it's time to shut that inner critic up for good.

In this chapter, we're diving deep into the art of building self-esteem so solid, even the harshest self-doubt won't stand a chance. You'll learn what self-esteem really is (spoiler: it's not about being perfect or having everyone's approval). More importantly, you'll discover practical strategies to silence that nagging voice in your head telling you you're not enough.

It's time for you to stop questioning your worth and start owning it. Because you're already enough. Let's make sure you believe it.

Explanation of Resilience-Building Methods

Let's talk about resilience—the magic that helps you bounce back when life hits the fan. At its core, resilience is your ability to adapt, recover, and even thrive in the face of challenges. And resilience doesn't just help you survive tough times—it helps you shine through them.

Resilience is the foundation of self-esteem because it reinforces the belief that you can handle whatever life throws at you. When you understand resilience, you realize it's not about avoiding struggles but about handling them with strength and grace. It's what turns a setback into a comeback and changes self-doubt into self-belief.

Why is this so vital for self-esteem? Because when you build resilience, you start to see challenges as opportunities to grow rather than as evidence that you're not good enough. Resilience reminds you that you're defined not by your failures but by how you rise after them.

So, exactly how does resilience fuel self-esteem?

- **Navigate challenges with confidence:** Resilience equips you with tools to face difficulties head-on. When you overcome obstacles—even small ones—you prove to yourself that you're capable. That proof creates an inner dialogue of encouragement rather than criticism. You start saying things like, "I handled that; I can handle this too."

- **Strengthen belief in yourself:** Every time you rise after a fall, you reinforce a powerful belief: *I can do hard things.* This belief is the cornerstone of unshakeable self-esteem. Resilience helps you trust in your ability to problem-solve, adapt, and move forward, no matter what happens.

- **Mitigate feelings of inadequacy:** Self-doubt has a way of creeping in during tough times. But when you create resilience, those feelings of inadequacy start losing their grip. Why? Because resilience shifts your focus from what went wrong to what you learned. Instead of spiraling into self-criticism, you develop self-compassion and a growth mindset.

Building resilience isn't about pretending everything's fine when it's not. It's about acknowledging your struggles while choosing to keep going anyway. It's the courage to say, "This is tough, but I'm tougher." Over time, building resilience doesn't just help you handle life's challenges—it actually changes how you see yourself. You start to recognize your strength, your adaptability, and your worth.

So, let's get started on building this powerful skill together. In the following exercise, you'll find practical strategies to strengthen your resilience, boost your confidence, and say goodbye to the nagging feelings of inadequacy that have been holding you back. Are you ready to amaze yourself with just how capable you really are?

Exercise: Building Resilience Through Practical Strategies

Identify Your Challenges

Start by reflecting on the specific challenges you're facing or have faced in the past. Write them down. This could be anything from personal setbacks to professional hurdles. Acknowledging these challenges is the first step in building resilience.

_____

_____

_____

_____

_____

_____

_____

_____

_____

_____

Problem-Solving Practice

Choose one challenge from your list and apply a problem-solving approach. Ask yourself the following questions:

- What's the challenge at hand?

_____

_____

_____

_____

- What are my possible options for addressing it?

_____

_____

_____

_____

- What resources or strengths do I have that can help me?

_____

_____

_____

- What's a small step I can take right now to move forward?

_____
_____
_____
_____
_____

Write down your answers to create a clear action plan. Remember, breaking down the problem into manageable steps can make it feel less overwhelming.

Develop a Support Network

Take a moment to evaluate your support network. Who are the people in your life that you can turn to during tough times? These could be friends, family members, mentors, or even support groups. Write down their names and consider reaching out to them, whether it's for advice, encouragement, or simply a listening ear.

_____
_____
_____

_____

_____

Connection Idea

Schedule a time to connect with someone from your support network. Share your feelings and challenges, and let them know how they can support you.

_____

_____

_____

_____

_____

Cultivate a Growth Mindset

Welcome the idea that challenges are opportunities for growth. Reflect on a recent challenge and write a short paragraph about what you've learned from it. How did it help you grow? How can this experience serve you in the future?

_____
_____
_____
_____
_____
_____
_____
_____
_____
_____

Embrace Challenges

Make a commitment to view challenges differently. Instead of seeing them as obstacles, try to see them as opportunities to boost your personal strength. When you face a new challenge, remind yourself of the skills you've developed and how you've overcome challenges in the past.

- **Affirmation:** Create an affirmation that reinforces this mindset. For example: "I welcome challenges because they help me become resilient and grow."

_____
_____
_____
_____
_____

Daily Resilience Practice

Incorporate a daily practice that builds resilience. This could be:

- journaling about your day and identifying moments of resilience or strength
- engaging in mindfulness or meditation to center yourself
- getting a daily intention that focuses on resilience, such as "I will face today's challenges with courage"

Reflect on Progress

At the end of each week, take a moment to reflect on your experiences:

- How have you applied these strategies?

_____
_____

- Have you noticed any shifts in your mindset or confidence levels?

_____
_____
_____
_____
_____

Journaling about these reflections can help reinforce your commitment to building resilience.

Remember, building resilience is a process—each step counts!

The Role of Mindset

Let's spill the tea: Your mindset is everything when it comes to resilience. It's like the DJ at the party of your life—spin the right tracks, and you're grooving through challenges like a boss. Spin the wrong ones, and you're stuck in a loop of "Why me?" So, let's dive into why a positive mindset changes everything for resilience and self-esteem.

The Magic of a Positive Mindset

- **Failures turned into fuel:** A positive mindset doesn't mean plastering on a fake smile and pretending everything's peachy. It's about choosing to see failures as stepping stones, not dead ends. Instead of "I'm terrible at this," you start saying, "That didn't work out, but what can I learn?" With this shift, every stumble becomes a chance to grow, not a reason to give up.

- **The optimism effect:** When you build optimism, you're more likely to take risks—good risks. You know, like going for that job you don't feel 100% qualified for (hint: nobody is) or finally putting yourself out there in a way that feels vulnerable but worth it. Optimism whispers, "What if it works out?" instead of screaming, "What if it doesn't?" And every leap you take feeds your self-esteem because it reminds you of your courage and capability.

- **Breaking free from validation nation:** Your self-worth isn't up for debate. It's not determined by your boss's feedback, your partner's mood, or how many likes your latest story got. When you accept a mindset that says, "I'm enough as I am," you stop outsourcing your worthiness. It's liberating, and it strengthens your resilience because you're no longer derailed by external noise.

Resilience in Action

Now, let's bring this to life with some real-world stories, because nothing beats seeing resilience in action:

- **Emma's leap of faith:** Emma had spent years doubting her ability to change careers until, one day, she decided to apply for a role outside her comfort zone. She didn't get it. Six months ago, this would have sent her spiraling. But instead, Emma used the feedback to refine her skills, applied again, and nailed it the second time. Her resilience not only landed her that dream job but gave her a new level of self-belief.

- **Maya's marathon:** Maya faced a rough breakup that left her questioning her worth. Two years ago when she'd faced a breakup she stayed in bed for weeks, not wanting to shower and binge-watching every rom-com in existence. This time, she processed her emotions and she took up running—starting with just a block at a time. Months later, she crossed the finish line of her first marathon, realizing she wasn't running from her past but toward her strength.

These stories remind us that resilience helps you thrive—and that boosts self-esteem like nothing else.

Here's where you come in. Take a moment to reflect: When was the last time you overcame something hard? Maybe you juggled a chaotic work week and still managed to show up for your friend. Maybe you spoke up when it felt uncomfortable. Whatever it was, own it! Every act of resilience, big or small, is a building block for your self-esteem.

Start jotting down your wins—yes, even the tiny ones. That time you didn't hit snooze for the third time? Write it down. The day you said no to something draining? Celebrate it. The more you acknowledge your resilience, the more you'll see just how strong and capable you are.

Because the truth is, resilience isn't just a skill—it's proof that you're unstoppable. And the more you welcome it, the more unshakeable your self-esteem becomes.

The Power of Gratitude Journaling

Sometimes, life feels like a never-ending loop of *ugh*. It's easy to get stuck in a cycle of noticing what's going wrong—missed deadlines, awkward interactions, or that mysterious sock thief who seems to live in your dryer. Enter gratitude journaling: your secret sauce for flipping the script and reclaiming your mindset. This isn't just about writing, "I'm thankful for my coffee" (though, let's be honest, coffee deserves its due); it's about rewiring your brain to focus on what's good, what's strong, and what's worth celebrating.

What Is Gratitude Journaling?

Gratitude journaling is exactly what it sounds like—taking a few moments each day to jot down the things you're grateful for. Big, small, or somewhere in between, these nuggets of goodness start to shift your perspective. Over time, this simple practice becomes a powerful tool for combating negative thoughts and building a more positive, resilient mindset.

Gratitude journaling doesn't just make you feel warm and fuzzy (though it definitely can). It helps you recognize your personal strengths, acknowledge your achievements, and create a sense of appreciation for the life you're creating. And when you focus on what's working, those nagging feelings of self-doubt don't stand a chance.

So, why does being grateful work?

- **A mental makeover:** Gratitude journaling is like a reset button for your brain. Instead of dwelling on what's lacking, you start noticing what's abundant. That mindset shift can make a huge difference when it comes to your self-esteem because you're training yourself to see value—in your life and in yourself.

- **Countering negative thought patterns:** Self-doubt can be loud. But gratitude journaling dials up the volume on positivity, effectively drowning out the negativity. Each time you reflect on what you're thankful for, you're rewiring your brain to focus on the good stuff, making it harder for those pesky self-critical thoughts to stick around.

- **Spotlight on strengths:** Gratitude journaling doesn't just highlight external blessings; it shines a light on you. Reflecting on your day often uncovers your own strengths—how you handled that tough conversation, how you made someone smile, or how you pushed through when it would've been easier to give up. Recognizing these wins reinforces your self-worth and builds your confidence.

The Benefits of Gratitude

Here's where things get even better: Practicing gratitude doesn't just boost your mood; it supercharges your resilience. Research shows that gratitude can enhance emotional coping skills, improve mental health, and even strengthen social connections (Diniz et al., 2023):

- **Improved mood and satisfaction:** Feeling stuck? Gratitude journaling is like a mood elevator, taking you from basement-level blahs to penthouse-level perspective. It's not magic; it's mindset. And the more satisfied you feel with life, the easier it is to believe in yourself.

- **Resilience on steroids:** Gratitude is the gift that keeps on giving—especially during tough times. By focusing on what's good, you build the mental muscle to handle challenges with grace and grit. Gratitude journaling reminds you that even when things feel hard, there's still light to be found.

- **Stronger connections:** Gratitude builds connection. When you regularly reflect on the people and moments that bring you joy, you naturally deepen those bonds. And knowing you're supported? That's a self-esteem booster if there ever was one.

Gratitude isn't just for your journal. Sharing it with others can supercharge its effects. Whether it's thanking a friend for their support, sending a note of appreciation to a mentor, or simply acknowledging someone's kindness, expressing gratitude strengthens relationships and builds community:

- **Self-esteem boost:** Expressing gratitude to others doesn't just make them feel good—it reminds you of the value you bring to their lives. Knowing you're part of a positive exchange reinforces your sense of worth and belonging.

- **Reflection and appreciation:** Sharing gratitude encourages you to reflect on the relationships that matter most. Who's shown up for you? Who's made a difference? Taking time to acknowledge these connections fosters deeper appreciation and mutual respect.

- **Creating a ripple effect:** Gratitude is contagious. By sharing it, you inspire others to do the same, creating a collective wave of positivity and support. For women especially, this shared gratitude can be a powerful reminder that we're stronger together.

Exercise: Starting Your Gratitude Journal

When you initiate and create a gratitude journal, you'll create a powerful tool for shifting your mindset, strengthening your sense of connection, and deepening your appreciation for life.

Gather Your Supplies

Begin by choosing a journal that feels inviting to you. It could be a beautiful notebook, a simple diary, or even a digital app—whatever resonates with you! Having a designated space for your gratitude practice will make it feel special.

Set a Consistent Time

Decide on a consistent time each day to dedicate to your gratitude journaling. Try starting your day on a positive note or end the evening by reflecting on your experiences. Setting this time helps make gratitude a part of your routine.

Start With Simple Prompts

Begin your journaling practice with simple prompts to guide your entries. Let's look at a few examples to get you started. Write just a sentence or two for each prompt while allowing your thoughts to flow naturally:

- What made me smile today?
- Who am I thankful for and why?
- What's one small pleasure I experienced this week?
- What challenges did I face, and what did I learn from them?

Note Big and Small Things

Encourage yourself to appreciate both the big achievements and the small joys in life. It could be anything from landing a big project at work to enjoying a warm cup of tea or having a good conversation with a friend. Recognizing these moments fosters a fuller appreciation of life.

Reflect on Your Entries

At the end of each week or month, take time to reflect on your gratitude entries:

- What patterns do you notice?

_____

_____

_____

- Are there recurring themes in what you're thankful for?

This reflection can deepen the impact of gratitude and enhance your overall mindset.

Explore Sharing Gratitude

Consider sharing your gratitude with others. Choose a few entries from your journal that you'd like to express gratitude for. You could write a heartfelt note, send a text, or even tell someone in person how much they mean to you.

- **Example:** "I want to thank you for being there when I needed support. Your kindness made a big difference in my day."

Positive Effects of Sharing

As you share your gratitude, pay attention to how it makes you feel. Noting the positive effects of expressing gratitude can reinforce your self-esteem and deepen your connections with others.

Reflect on Relationships

Use your gratitude practice to reflect on your relationships. Who lifts you up in your life? Identify and appreciate them in your journal, and consider ways to express your appreciation directly.

Collective Gratitude

Encourage a sense of community by sharing gratitude with a group of friends or family. Start a gratitude circle where everyone takes turns expressing what they're grateful for. Collective gratitude can enhance connections among women and strengthen ties within your community.

Enjoy the journey of gratitude!

Utilizing Positive Self-Reflection for Self-Esteem Enhancement

We're often our own toughest critics, dwelling on our missteps while brushing off our victories like they don't count. Positive self-reflection flips that script. It's the practice of pausing, looking inward, and giving yourself credit where credit's due. And there's a lot you deserve credit for.

What Is Positive Self-Reflection?

Positive self-reflection is about focusing on your strengths, accomplishments, and growth rather than fixating on your flaws. It's not about inflating your ego; it's about acknowledging your worth and seeing yourself clearly—without the filter of self-doubt or external validation.

So, why does positive self-reflection matter? Let's break it down:

- **Spotlights your strengths:** Taking time to reflect on what you've done well helps you recognize your unique talents and abilities. Whether it's how you handled a tough day or how you made someone smile, these moments are proof of your capability.

- **Builds self-worth from within:** When you reflect positively, you shift your focus away from what others think of you and toward what *you* value about yourself. This internal validation fosters a stronger, more resilient sense of self-worth.

- **Calms negative thoughts:** Negative thoughts love to crash the party. Positive self-reflection acts as a bouncer, redirecting those thoughts by grounding you in the reality of your strengths and achievements. The result? A calmer, more confident you.

Positive self-reflection isn't about perfection—it's about perspective. By making it a regular practice, you'll not only strengthen your self-esteem but also create a deeper connection with yourself.

Exercise: Methods for Effective Self-Reflection

When you incorporate these methods for effective self-reflection into your daily life, you'll create a valuable practice that creates ongoing self-awareness and personal growth.

Set the Stage for Reflection

Begin by creating a comfortable space for self-reflection. Find a quiet spot where you feel relaxed and free from distractions. This will be different for everyone. It might be a comfortable chair, a calm corner in your home, or even a spot in a park surrounded by nature.

End-of-Day Review

Incorporate a simple end-of-day review into your routine. Take a few moments before bed to reflect on your day. Ask yourself these questions:

- What went well today?

_____
_____
_____
_____
_____

- What challenges did I face, and how did I respond?

_____
_____
_____
_____

- What am I grateful for that happened today?

_____
_____
_____
_____

Set Specific Reflection Goals

Write down specific goals for your self-reflection practice. These goals can guide your personal growth and give direction to your reflections.

- Example goals:
    - "I want to understand my reactions to stress better."
    - "I'd like to track my progress in handling negative beliefs."

- Write these goals down and revisit them regularly to assess your growth.

_____
_____
_____
_____
_____

Daily Journaling

Dedicate time each day or week to journal your thoughts and feelings. This practice can clarify your experiences and reactions, helping you uncover insights about yourself.

- Start with prompts such as:
    - How did I feel when faced with a challenge today?
    - What thoughts crossed my mind that I want to explore further?
    - What emotions surfaced during my interactions with others?

Practice Mindfulness

Incorporate mindfulness techniques to enhance your self-reflection. Spend a few minutes focusing on your breath, observing your thoughts without judgment. This can help you become more aware of your feelings and set the stage for deeper reflection.

Weekly Reflection Sessions

Schedule a weekly reflection session where you can dedicate more time to self-analysis. Choose a quiet evening or weekend morning to sit down with your journal. Review your entries from the week, noting any patterns, revelations, or areas you'd like to explore further.

Recognize Growth

As you engage in self-reflection, take time to acknowledge your growth and progress. Note any positive changes in your mindset or behavior, and celebrate these victories—no matter how small.

Share Reflections With a Trusted Friend

Consider sharing your insights with a trusted friend or mentor. Discussing your reflections can deepen your understanding and provide new perspectives. It can also create connection and support as you embark on your personal growth journey.

From resilience to gratitude to positive self-reflection, you now have a powerful tool kit to rewrite the narrative you tell yourself. It's not about being perfect or bulletproof—it's about recognizing your worth, embracing your strengths, and showing up for yourself, flaws and all.

Now that you've started to build your self-esteem, it's time to take things up a notch. In the next chapter, we'll dive into the confidence mindset—the key to stepping into any room (or situation) like you belong there, because guess what? You absolutely do. See you in the next chapter!

Chapter 5:

The Confidence Mindset

This chapter is about more than just feeling good in the moment. It's about adopting a mindset that builds confidence—not the fleeting kind that depends on external validation, but the steady, unshakable belief in who you are and what you can accomplish. Confidence isn't a magic trick or something other people just have. It's a skill that can be learned, practiced, and strengthened.

It's time to challenge that inner critic, step away from the self-doubt that's been holding you back, and plant some seeds of self-assurance. By the end of this chapter, you'll have practical strategies to start showing up for yourself with the same energy and support you'd give your best friend. Let's do this.

Differentiating Confidence From Competence

Let's clear something up: Confidence and competence aren't interchangeable, but together, they're a powerful duo. Understanding the difference between the two—and how they work together—can change everything in your personal growth journey.

Defining Confidence

Confidence is that spark within you—the belief that you can do something, even if you're not an expert yet. You don't need to know every detail or have all the answers. You just need to trust yourself and your ability to figure life out along the way. Confidence gives you the courage to take risks, try new things, and push outside your comfort zone. It says, "I may not have it all figured out, but I believe in my ability to learn and grow."

Think about it: If you waited until you felt 100% ready for every challenge, how many opportunities would you miss? Confidence lets you leap into the unknown, even when your skill set is still catching up. And the more risks you take, the more your confidence grows, creating opportunities for new adventures in both your personal and professional life.

Understanding Competence

Now, competence is the steady foundation under that leap of faith. It's the actual skills, knowledge, and abilities you've developed over time. Competence grows through experience—showing up, learning, practicing, and sometimes failing before trying again. Unlike confidence, which lives in your mindset, competence is tangible. It's proof of your dedication and hard work.

When you acknowledge your competencies, you fuel your confidence. It's like saying, "I've done this before, so I know I can handle it." But competence isn't static. It grows as you take on new challenges and commit to self-improvement.

The Interplay Between Confidence and Competence

It's important to understand that confidence and competence are a feedback loop. Confidence empowers you to take action—even when your competence isn't fully developed yet. Every time you step up and try, you gain experience and build competence. In turn, that competence reinforces your confidence, creating a cycle of growth.

But balance is key. Overconfidence without the necessary competence can lead to rash decisions, while competence without confidence can leave you paralyzed by self-doubt. When you align the two, you create a dynamic force that propels you forward with clarity and purpose.

So, here's the takeaway: Confidence and competence aren't opposing forces; they're teammates. Accepting both means believing in yourself enough to start and trusting the process enough to grow. And when you do? That's when the real change happens.

Exercise: Cultivating Confidence and Competence

When you actively engage in this exercise to build confidence and competence, you'll empower yourself to take on new challenges and grow both personally and professionally.

Define Your Goals

Start by identifying specific personal and professional goals that you want to achieve. Make sure these goals are achievable and relevant to your growth. Write them down.

- **Example goals:**
    - **Personal goal:** "I want to learn a new skill, like painting or cooking."
    - **Professional goal:** "I aim to improve my public speaking skills before the next team meeting."

_____
_____
_____

Set Incremental Steps

Break down each goal into smaller, actionable steps. This makes them feel less overwhelming and allows you to track your progress more easily.

- **Example for the personal goal:**
    - Research a painting class or online tutorials.
    - Commit to practicing for 30 minutes twice a week.
- **Example for the professional goal:**
    - Attend a public speaking workshop.
    - Practice presenting in front of a friend or family member.

_____
_____
_____
_____
_____
_____
_____
_____
_____
_____
_____
_____
_____
_____

Seek Out Challenges

Welcome opportunities that push you out of your comfort zone. Keep looking for challenges that align with your goals, as this will help you build both your confidence and competence.

- Consider participating in community events, taking on new responsibilities at work, or joining clubs that involve skills you wish to develop.

Document Your Experiences

Keep a record of your journey. After each challenge or new experience, take time to write down how it went. Reflecting on these experiences reinforces your growth and can boost both your confidence and your competence.

- What did you learn?

_____
_____
_____
_____
_____

- How did it feel to tackle the challenge?

_____
_____
_____

Reflect on Past Successes

Take a moment to reflect on past successes where you overcame challenges and gained competence. Write about these experiences, focusing on what you learned and how they contributed to your confidence.

- Remember times when you stepped outside your comfort zone and succeeded, no matter how small the victory may seem. These reflections serve as powerful reminders of what you're capable of achieving.

_____
_____
_____
_____
_____
_____
_____
_____
_____
_____

Create a Confidence Board

Consider crafting a visual representation of your achievements. This can be a physical board or a digital collage. Include motivational quotes, photos of past successes, or even snippets of positive feedback from others.

- Place this board somewhere you can see it daily as a reminder of your capabilities and growth.

Celebrate Your Journey

As you complete each step or achieve each goal, take time to celebrate your progress. This could be as simple as treating yourself to a small reward or sharing your success with friends and family. Celebrating your achievements reinforces the connection between effort and success.

Establish a Supportive Network

Surround yourself with supportive individuals who uplift and encourage you on your journey. Share your goals with them and seek their feedback and encouragement. Engaging with a community can bolster both your confidence and your competence.

Welcome the journey, and remember that every step you take is a massive achievement!

Practicing the Power Pose

Confidence isn't just about what's in your mind—it's also in how you carry yourself. Enter power posing, a simple yet powerful way to supercharge your confidence before tackling life's challenges. Let's break it down so you can start using this tool today.

Power posing is about using your body to influence how you feel. Standing tall, spreading out, and holding postures of confidence can physically and psychologically shift your state. Research suggests that power poses may elevate testosterone (the "confidence hormone") while lowering cortisol (the "stress hormone"), helping you feel more assured and in control (Elsesser, 2020).

Even small changes, like lifting your chin or planting your feet firmly on the ground, can create a huge shift in how you perceive yourself and approach the world. Incorporating power poses into your routine can change how you prepare for stressful moments—think job interviews, public speaking, or tough conversations.

Practical Instructions for Power Posing

Ready to give it a try? Here's how to make power posing work for you (Miles, 2023):

1. **Choose your pose:**
    - **The superwoman:** Stand tall with your feet shoulder-width apart, hands on hips, and chest slightly lifted.
    - **The victory pose:** Raise your arms high above your head like you've just won a race.
    - **The desk boss:** Lean forward slightly, hands firmly on a desk or table, projecting authority.
2. **Hold the pose:** Stay in position for one to two minutes. This might feel a little awkward at first, but trust the process—your body and mind are aligning.
3. **Breathe and visualize:** As you hold your pose, take deep breaths and visualize success in whatever you're about to do.
4. **Incorporate it:** Practice power posing before important events or whenever you need an extra boost. With time, it can become second nature.

The Science Behind It

You might be wondering, *Does this really work?* According to research, the answer is yes. Studies have shown that our body language not only reflects our emotional state but also influences it (Elsesser, 2020). When you adopt expansive, open poses, you can actively shape your mental state to feel more confident and capable.

For example, a groundbreaking study highlighted how people who practiced power poses before a stressful task experienced lower anxiety and improved performance compared to those who didn't (Weineck et al., 2020). While science is still exploring the full effects of physical posture, many agree that it plays a crucial role in shaping our thoughts and emotions.

Incorporating Power Posing Into Daily Life

Power posing doesn't have to be reserved for big moments; it can become a daily habit to reinforce confidence. Here are some simple ways to integrate it:

- **Morning ritual:** Start your day with a power pose while setting an intention or reciting a daily affirmation.

- **Pre-challenge prep:** Take a moment to power pose before meetings, presentations, or other high-pressure situations.

- **Daily boost:** Use power posing whenever you feel your confidence waver. Commit to even 30 seconds to see a difference.

- **Share the practice:** Teach power posing to friends, family, or coworkers. There's power in shared confidence.

Power posing is more than just a physical exercise—it's a mindset shift. It's about taking control of your body to influence your emotions and actions positively. So, the next time self-doubt creeps in, remember this: Stand tall, own your space, and let your posture pave the way to confidence.

Rewriting Negative Thoughts Into Empowering Statements

Your thoughts are powerful—they shape how you see yourself and the world. Unfortunately, negative self-talk can find its way in, undermining your confidence and keeping you stuck in doubt. But remember, you have the ability to rewrite those thoughts into empowering statements that uplift and inspire you.

The first step to change is awareness. Negative self-talk often masquerades as "truth," but when you start listening closely, you'll notice patterns that chip away at your confidence.

Recognizing these thoughts isn't about judging yourself—it's about shining a light on what's been hiding in the shadows. Start by keeping a log of your negative thoughts. Jot them down when they arise, and notice when they tend to show up (e.g., before a big decision, after a mistake, or when comparing yourself to others). Awareness is the key to change.

The Impact of Reframed Thoughts

Reframing your thoughts isn't just a mental exercise—it's a transformative practice that can ripple through every area of your life. By replacing self-defeating narratives with positive, empowering ones, you're changing your mindset and shaping your emotional well-being, resilience, and confidence. Let's explore the profound effects of this practice.

Positive self-statements have a direct impact on your emotional state. When you consistently challenge and reframe negative thoughts, you:

- **Reduce stress:** Positive thoughts decrease the physiological stress response, helping you feel calmer and more in control (Mayo Clinic Staff, 2023).

- **Boost optimism:** Affirming your strengths and potential makes you more likely to see challenges as opportunities instead of obstacles.

- **Enhance emotional well-being:** Positive self-talk creates self-compassion, which improves mood and overall happiness (Grzybowski & Brinthaupt, 2022).

Research supports this. Studies on positive affirmations show that repeating empowering statements can reduce stress, increase self-esteem, and improve problem-solving abilities (Grzybowski & Brinthaupt, 2022). Brain imaging research even reveals that affirmations activate areas of the brain associated with self-worth and positive emotion (Cascio et al., 2016).

Exercise: Building a Habit of Reframing Negative Thoughts

When you build a habit of reframing negative thoughts into empowering affirmations, you cultivate a more positive mindset and strengthen your overall confidence.

Establish a Routine

To make reframing a regular practice, it's essential to establish a routine that fits seamlessly into your daily life. Choose a specific time each day when you can dedicate a few minutes to this practice. Maybe during your morning coffee works, or mid-afternoon—or right before bed may even work better? Regardless, consistency is key!

Create Daily Affirmations

Write down daily affirmations that align with your personal goals and values. These should be short, positive statements that reflect the mindset you want to cultivate. Here are a few examples to get you started:

- "I am capable of overcoming challenges."
- "I embrace new opportunities for growth."
- "I trust myself to make the right decisions."

_____
_____
_____
_____
_____

Integrate Gratitude

Incorporate gratitude into your reframing practice. Take time daily to jot down three things that make you grateful. They can be big or small—anything from a supportive friend to a delicious meal you enjoyed. Gratitude strengthens the way you think positively and takes your focus away from negativity.

Combine Practices

Enhance your reframing practice by combining it with your gratitude journaling. For example, when you write down your daily affirmations, follow up with your gratitude entries. You might say, "I am capable of overcoming challenges," followed by, "I am grateful for the support of my friends." This combination strengthens both your mindset and your emotional well-being.

Track Your Progress

Keep a journal or log to track changes in your mood and confidence as you practice reframing. Each week, jot down reflections on how you've felt throughout the week. This tracking allows you to observe patterns and improvements over time, reinforcing the effectiveness of your practice:

- Have you noticed a shift in your mindset?

- Do you feel more empowered to tackle challenges?

- What instances can you recall where applying reframing made a difference in your day?

Set Monthly Check-Ins

At the end of each month, take time to review your reflections and track your growth. What affirmations resonated most? How did your mood and confidence evolve? Celebrate any progress you've made, big or small, as a way to motivate yourself to keep going.

When you recognize negative self-talk, rewrite it into empowering statements, and make this practice a habit, you're not just changing how you think; you're changing how you show up in the world. Every reframe is a step toward resilience, self-assurance, and a mindset that empowers you to thrive.

But let's be honest—no matter how confident you become, the fear of judgment can still creep in. Maybe you worry about what others think or hold back your true self. That fear can be a roadblock to your growth. In the next chapter, we'll dive into overcoming the fear of judgment so you can step boldly into your life, unshaken by others' opinions. It's time to silence that inner critic and welcome the freedom to be unapologetically you.

Chapter 6:

Overcoming the Fear of Judgment

Do you feel that a fear of judgment is holding you back? Maybe you hesitate to share your opinion in a meeting, post that picture you love, or even wear that outfit that feels *so* you. You're not alone. The fear of being judged is a voice whispering that you're "less than," convincing you that everyone around you is secretly critiquing your every move.

In this chapter, we're diving into why the fear of judgment exists, how it shows up in your life, and, most importantly, how to stop it from stealing your joy. You'll learn real strategies to quiet the noise, build unshakable confidence, and step into your life like the badass you are—because you're enough, just as you are. Let's kick fear to the curb and focus on your voice, your dreams, and your truth.

Evolutionary and Personal Roots of the Fear of Judgment

Why does the fear of judgment feel so powerful, like it's stitched into the fabric of who you are? Because, in many ways, it is. To truly overcome it, we need to take a journey back—back to the days of survival-driven instincts and the personal stories that shaped your sense of self.

Humans are wired to belong. Thousands of years ago, being part of a group wasn't just a nice to have; it was a matter of survival. Being accepted by your tribe meant safety, access to resources, and protection from predators. Judgment—real or perceived—was a signal that you might be pushed out, left vulnerable to the dangers of the wild.

Fast forward to today, and your brain hasn't fully caught on that the stakes are no longer life or death. That anxious knot in your stomach when you feel judged? It's your brain's outdated survival mechanism kicking in. Recognizing that this fear is instinctual, not personal, is a game-changer. It's not about being "less than"—it's about your brain doing what it thinks it needs to do to keep you safe.

Personal Experiences: Stories That Stick

While evolution laid the groundwork, your personal experiences built the structure. Maybe you were criticized for your appearance as a teenager or dismissed when you shared your ideas. These moments leave a mark, often creating a script that whispers, "Don't take up too much space; they'll judge you."

But the empowering truth is that you can rewrite that script. Start by reflecting on those formative experiences. Where did your fear of judgment begin? Acknowledge the pain but also remind yourself that you've grown. You're not the same person who faced those moments, and their power over you doesn't have to last forever.

And remember, everyone has felt judged at some point. Recognizing that judgment is universal creates connection, not isolation. You're not alone in this—far from it.

As if evolution and personal stories weren't enough, society adds its own layer of expectations. The "perfect woman" myth—flawless, selfless, always on top of everything—has set an impossible standard. No wonder the fear of judgment thrives in a world that constantly tells us we're not measuring up.

But those standards are built on shaky ground. They're arbitrary, shifting, and deeply flawed. Challenging them is an act of rebellion and self-love. When you embrace your unique qualities and reject narrow definitions of worth, you free yourself and pave the way for others to do the same.

The Power of Narratives: Rewriting Your Story

The stories you tell yourself matter. If your internal dialogue is filled with "I'll never be good enough," it's time for a rewrite. Shifting from negative self-talk to affirming, empowering narratives is like hitting reset on how you view yourself.

And when you share your story, scars and all, it helps you and it helps others. Vulnerability creates connection. It validates that fear of judgment is real but also conquerable. This is why I decided to write this workbook. Together, we can dismantle the power fear of judgment holds over us.

When you understand where your fear of judgment comes from—evolution, personal experiences, cultural standards—you move toward breaking free from it. You're not bound by the past or by society's expectations. You have the power to rewrite your story (I did), accept your authenticity, and live unapologetically. Because you're perfect, just as you are.

Journaling to Identify Judgment Patterns

If fear of judgment feels like an unwelcome guest showing up at all the wrong moments, journaling can help you figure out where it's coming from and how to stop inviting it in. Think of a journal as your personal Sherlock Holmes, quietly uncovering the clues behind your feelings of judgment, helping you see patterns that might otherwise stay hidden.

Creating a Judgment Journal: A Tool for Awareness

Sometimes, the fear of judgment feels so automatic that we don't stop to ask, "Where is this coming from?" A dedicated judgment journal gives you the space to pause and reflect. By jotting down specific moments when you felt judged, you can start connecting the dots. Maybe it's a particular environment, a specific person, or even certain types of conversations that make you feel most vulnerable.

The simple act of naming your emotions in real time—"I felt dismissed in the meeting" or "Their comment made me feel small"—builds self-awareness. It's not about judging yourself for feeling judged (let's not go down that rabbit hole!) but about observing your emotional landscape with curiosity and compassion.

Prompting Reflection: Asking the Right Questions

Sometimes, it's hard to know where to start with journaling. That's where prompts come in. Reflecting on specific questions about your experiences with judgment can be incredibly revealing. They might help you explore moments when you felt seen and valued, as well as times when you felt dismissed or criticized. Both sides of the coin are worth exploring because they show you what triggers you and what uplifts you.

The more you dig into these experiences, the clearer the picture becomes. You start to notice themes—not just about what others say or do, but about how you respond. These insights aren't just "aha!" moments; they're the seeds of actionable change.

Reviewing Patterns: Spotting the Recurring Themes

When you regularly review your journal entries, patterns start to emerge. Maybe you notice that you feel most judged in professional settings or around a particular friend. Or maybe it's an internal critic whispering harsh words when things don't go as planned.

Recognizing these patterns allows you to anticipate judgment-heavy situations and prepare for them. But it also shows you where you've grown. Over time, you might notice that the sting of a critical comment doesn't last as long or that you're quicker to shake off unnecessary worry.

This clarity is a superpower, helping you approach moments of potential judgment with more confidence and less fear.

Visualization Techniques: Adding Depth to Reflection

Journaling doesn't have to stop with words. Pairing it with visualization techniques can add a deeper layer of understanding. Imagine what your life might feel like without the constant hum of judgment—how much lighter, freer, and more vibrant you'd feel. Or picture yourself standing strong in the face of judgment, unshaken by criticism, confident in your worth.

These visual exercises work hand in hand with journaling to create a full picture of your relationship with judgment and how to change it. They're like mental rehearsals for stepping into a life where fear of judgment no longer calls the shots.

Journaling is a way to hold a mirror up to your thoughts and emotions. It gives you the tools to understand where your fear of judgment comes from, what keeps it alive, and how you can begin to release its grip. As you reflect, patterns will emerge, insights will unfold, and you'll find yourself stepping into your power, one journal entry at a time.

Exercise: Journaling to Identify Judgment Patterns

When you actively engage in this exercise to identify judgment patterns through journaling, you'll develop a deeper understanding of your emotional landscape.

Create a Judgment Journal

Begin by dedicating a journal specifically for tracking instances of feeling judged. Choose a format that feels comfortable to you—whether it's a small notebook, a digital app, or even a simple document on your computer. The act of writing in a designated space can create a sense of purpose and focus.

Acknowledge Feelings in Real Time

Whenever you notice feelings of judgment throughout the day, make a note of them in your journal. Try to capture these instances as they happen, allowing yourself to express your emotional reactions honestly.

- Ask yourself: What triggered this feeling? How did I respond?

This practice promotes self-awareness and honest reflection.

Document Specific Situations

Write down details about the situations that triggered these feelings of judgment. Include information such as:

- the context (e.g., social gathering, workplace, online interaction)
- who was involved
- what was said or done that made you feel judged
- your immediate emotional response

This specificity helps you identify recurring themes and triggers in your emotional landscape.

Utilize Targeted Reflection Prompts

Use targeted prompts to guide your journaling sessions and deepen your exploration. Here are some prompts to consider:

- Write about a recent experience when you felt judged. What were the circumstances, and how did the experience affect you?

- Reflect on a time when you judged yourself harshly. What triggered that judgment, and how can you reframe it?

- Identify positive experiences where you felt accepted or appreciated. What made those moments feel safe?

Engaging with these prompts can spark insights and generate actionable responses related to your feelings about judgment.

Analyze Your Responses

After writing, take some time to analyze your responses. Look for common themes or underlying thoughts that emerge. Ask yourself:

- What patterns do I notice in how I react to feelings of judgment?

- Are there specific situations that tend to trigger these feelings?

- What beliefs about myself are influencing my reactions?

This analysis can yield insights that help you develop strategies for managing future judgments.

Regularly Review Patterns

Set aside time each week or month to review your journal entries. During these sessions, look for trends in your feelings of judgment over time. Ask yourself:

- Are there certain people, situations, or environments that consistently trigger feelings of judgment?

- How do my responses change based on perceived judgments?

This recognition allows you to anticipate and prepare for situations that may incite fear, empowering you to take proactive steps.

Incorporate Visualization Techniques

Boost your journaling practice by combining it with visualization techniques. Begin by finding a quiet moment to close your eyes and imagine scenarios where judgment is absent:

- Visualize yourself in situations that typically induce judgment, but this time imagine feeling completely at ease and confident. Allow yourself to welcome a sense of safety.

- Similarly, practice visualizing your strength in dealing with judgment. Picture yourself responding positively and resiliently, reinforcing your confidence.

This practice empowers you to manage fears related to judgment and create a more positive self-perception. Enjoy your journey of self-discovery!

Methods of Self-Evaluation for Personal Judgments

How often do you find yourself being your own harshest critic, nitpicking every little thing you say or do? It's exhausting, isn't it? The truth is, personal judgments often hold us back far more than external ones ever could. But with the right tools, you can shift your perspective, quiet that inner critic, and nurture self-acceptance. Let's explore how self-evaluation can help you break free.

Self-Assessment Techniques: Getting Clear on the Inner Critic

One of the first steps in tackling personal judgments is recognizing them. Start by asking yourself: "Is my self-talk aligned with who I really am, or am I holding myself to impossible standards?" Regular check-ins can help. These might be as simple as jotting down your thoughts during moments of self-doubt or using a checklist to evaluate whether your self-judgments are based on facts or assumptions.

Another powerful tool is clarifying your values and personal standards. When you define what truly matters to you, it becomes easier to filter out the noise of unnecessary self-criticism. Aligning your self-evaluations with your authentic values helps you judge yourself on what *you* deem important, not on arbitrary external expectations.

And when negative self-assessments creep in, don't let them settle. Challenge them with constructive questions like: "Is this criticism helpful or just harsh? What can I learn from this?" Growth doesn't come from tearing yourself down but from building yourself up with clarity and compassion.

Exercise: Creating a Judgment Detox Plan

Creating and implementing a judgment detox plan, you empower yourself to manage self-judgment sustainably and build a more compassionate inner dialogue.

Understanding Self-Judgment

Begin by reflecting on what self-judgment means to you. Spend a few moments writing down how self-judgment manifests in your life:

- What thoughts do you find yourself repeating?

_____

_____

_____

_____
_____

- How do these judgments affect your self-esteem and overall well-being?

_____
_____
_____
_____
_____

Acknowledging the impact of self-judgment is the first step toward cultivating self-compassion.

Identify Your Triggers

Take some time to pinpoint situations or experiences that trigger your self-judgment. Here are some questions to consider:

- In which areas of your life do you tend to be the hardest on yourself?

_____
_____
_____
_____
_____

- Are there specific people, settings, or events that intensify your self-critical thoughts?

_____
_____
_____
_____
_____

- How does your inner dialogue change in these moments? Document these triggers to create a clearer understanding of what leads to self-judgment.

_____
_____
_____

Create Compassionate Alternatives

For each self-judgment trigger you've identified, brainstorm a compassionate alternative. Focus on how you would talk to a friend or someone you care about in similar situations:

- Instead of "I always mess up," try "I'm doing my best, and mistakes are a part of my growth."

- Instead of "I'm not good enough," remind yourself, "I'm enough just as I am."

Write down these alternative statements next to your triggers for easy reference.

Develop Strategies for Reduction

Look at the list of triggers and compassionate alternatives you've created. For each trigger, develop at least one strategy to reduce its impact. Consider these ideas:

- **Mindfulness:** Use mindfulness techniques to remain present and aware of your thoughts when you feel self-judgment creeping in.

- **Cognitive restructuring:** Challenge negative thoughts by asking yourself if they're based on facts or assumptions.

- **Affirmation practice:** Repeat your compassionate alternatives as affirmations, especially when you feel self-judgment arising.

Create a Commitment Statement

Write a personal commitment statement that outlines your intention to decrease self-judgment behaviors. This can serve as a motivational reminder on your journey toward self-compassion. Here's an example to inspire you:

- "I commit to treating myself with kindness, embracing my imperfections, and practicing self-acceptance daily."

Place your commitment statement somewhere visible, such as on your mirror or at your workspace, to keep it front of mind.

_____

_____

Implement your Judgment Detox Plan

Take action by implementing your plan. When you encounter feelings of self-judgment, pause and refer back to your triggers and compassionate alternatives. Use the strategies you've developed to manage those feelings effectively.

Regular Check-Ins

Schedule regular check-ins with yourself—perhaps weekly or biweekly—to assess your progress:

- How have you been managing self-judgment?

_____
_____
_____
_____
_____

- Are there new triggers you've identified?

_____
_____
_____
_____
_____

Reflect on the effectiveness of your strategies and adjust them as needed.

Celebrate Progress

Acknowledge your efforts and celebrate any progress you make. Consider keeping a journal of your successes along the way, noting how your feelings toward self-judgment have shifted.

Welcome this journey, knowing that you're worthy of kindness and acceptance!

Positive Affirmation Alternatives: Flipping the Script

Self-judgment often thrives on a loop of negative self-talk. The antidote? Positive affirmations. These aren't just fluffy phrases—they're intentional statements that remind you of your worth, value, and strength. Imagine replacing thoughts like *I don't deserve love and respect* with affirmations like "I am learning and growing every day."

Creating a list of affirmations tailored to your struggles can provide a counterbalance to that inner critic. But the key isn't just writing them down—it's practicing them. Repetition builds belief. Maybe you whisper them to yourself in the mirror every morning or jot them in a journal before bed. These small rituals anchor positivity in your daily life and gradually rewire how you see yourself.

Seeking External Feedback: Seeing Yourself Through Kinder Eyes

Sometimes, you're too close to the problem to see the truth. That's where trusted friends, mentors, or even coaches come in. They can help you uncover strengths you might overlook and reframe criticisms that feel overwhelming.

External feedback isn't about validation—it's about perspective. The people who genuinely care about you can provide clarity, pointing out where you might be too hard on yourself or helping you celebrate the wins you tend to downplay. Vulnerably sharing your struggles with judgment can also foster deeper connections. You might discover that others feel the same way, creating a shared space for mutual growth.

And here's the beautiful part: As you allow others to see the real you, flaws and all, you'll start to see yourself in a kinder, more forgiving light. You're not defined by your judgments—you're defined by how you rise above them. It's time to move on to the next chapter, where we dive into the topic of overthinking!

Chapter 7:

Breaking Free From the Cycle of Overthinking

Have you ever found yourself replaying a conversation for the tenth time, picking apart every word you said, convinced they must think you're ridiculous? Or maybe you've stayed up late, staring at the ceiling, spiraling through a hundred what-ifs about tomorrow. If you can relate, you're not alone. Overthinking has a way of convincing us that dissecting every detail will somehow make us feel better or more prepared, but instead, it leaves us feeling drained, anxious, and stuck.

Overthinking isn't solving your problems; it's just stealing your peace. This chapter is here to help you break that cycle. By the end, you'll not only know how to quiet that overthinking brain of yours; you'll feel empowered to reclaim your time, your energy, and your joy.

You are so much more than the stories your mind spins. Let's break free and move forward—together.

Keeping a Gratitude Journal for Positive Reinforcement

Gratitude shifts your focus from what's going wrong to what's going right. When you're caught in the cycle of overthinking, gratitude acts like a reset button, gently pulling you out of your mental maze and grounding you in what matters most. It's time to explore how practicing gratitude, specifically through journaling, can be a powerful tool to counter negative self-talk and create a more positive outlook.

Gratitude is about intentionally recognizing the good in your life. When you focus on gratitude, your brain starts to shift its attention away from the negatives and toward the positives. Over time, this practice can boost your mental well-being, helping you create a mindset that's more resilient and optimistic. And gratitude isn't just about you—it has a ripple effect. Sharing your gratitude with others strengthens your relationships and fosters deeper connections, creating a positive cycle that benefits everyone.

Daily Gratitude Practices

Incorporating gratitude into your daily routine is a simple yet impactful way to build a habit of positivity. Whether it's starting your morning with a moment of reflection or ending your day by noting what went well, gratitude can anchor your day with a sense of calm and contentment. These small, consistent practices can create space in your mind for joy and help you reclaim moments that might otherwise be lost to worry or self-doubt.

Gratitude has a unique ability to interrupt the loops of overthinking that can take over your thoughts. When your mind is stuck on what could go wrong, gratitude helps you focus on what's gone right. It reminds you of the good things that persist, even when life feels overwhelming. Gratitude also nurtures resilience, giving you the mental strength to handle stress and uncertainty without letting it spiral out of control.

Gratitude becomes even more powerful when it's shared. Expressing your appreciation to others creates positive feedback loops in your relationships, deepens trust, and diminishes feelings of isolation. When you acknowledge what others bring to your life, it strengthens those connections, encouraging a sense of mutual support and understanding. And when you inspire others to practice gratitude, you're contributing to a collective sense of well-being that benefits everyone around you.

Gratitude can change your perspective, your relationships, and your overall mental well-being. In the following exercise, you'll learn how to use journaling as a tool for gratitude, giving you a practical way to reinforce positivity and break free from the overthinking cycle.

Exercise: Daily Gratitude Practices

When you integrate these daily gratitude practices into your life, you'll create a habit of positivity that fosters resilience and strengthens your connections.

Incorporate Daily Gratitude Prompts

Start by setting a simple daily prompt for yourself. Choose a time each day—perhaps in the morning or during lunch—when you can reflect on what you're grateful for. Create a list of prompts to guide your reflection. Here are some examples:

- What's one thing I appreciated about myself today?
- Who made my day better, and how?
- What small pleasure brought me joy recently?

_____

_____

_____

_____
_____
_____
_____

Morning Gratitude Routine

Begin each day with a positivity-focused morning routine centered around gratitude. When you wake up, take a few moments to think about three things you're grateful for. It could be the warmth of your bed, the sound of birds outside, or a supportive friend. Envision how these things set a positive tone for your day. Consider reciting them out loud or writing them down to cement the positive feelings.

_____
_____
_____
_____
_____
_____
_____
_____
_____

Evening Reflections

Create a calming evening ritual where you reflect on your day. Before going to bed, take five minutes to jot down three things that went well during the day, no matter how small. This practice fosters a sense of closure and positivity, helping you wind down on a positive note.

- Ask yourself: "What did I learn today? How did I overcome a challenge?"

_____
_____
_____
_____
_____
_____
_____
_____
_____

Transforming Overthinking With Gratitude

When you find yourself overthinking or getting caught up in negative thought loops, pause and shift your focus to gratitude. Make a conscious effort to redirect your thoughts by recognizing at least three things you're thankful for at that moment.

- Example: If you're worrying about an upcoming presentation, remind yourself of the preparation you've done, the support of your friends, and the opportunity to learn and grow.

_____
_____
_____

_____
_____
_____
_____
_____
_____
_____

Writing for Mental Reset

Whenever you feel overwhelmed or stressed, take a moment to write down three things you're grateful for. This small act can serve as a powerful mental reset, shifting your perspective from negativity to appreciation.

The Power of Sharing Gratitude

Explore the impact of expressing gratitude toward others. Make it a point to share your feelings of appreciation with at least one person each week. Whether it's a heartfelt message, a note, or an in-person conversation, expressing gratitude can enhance your relationships and create a positive feedback loop.

- Example: "I wanted to thank you for always being there for me. Your support means the world to me."

Deepening Connections Through Sharing

As you express gratitude, pay attention to how it impacts your relationships. Share your observations about how appreciation strengthens your connections with others. You might find that expressing gratitude diminishes feelings of isolation and fosters a sense of community.

Encourage Collective Gratitude

Consider organizing a gratitude practice with friends, family, or coworkers. This could be a weekly gathering where everyone shares what they're grateful for, creating a collective well-being boost. Encourage others to start their own gratitude journals or share prompts to enhance the experience together.

Welcome the path of gratitude; it has the power to change your mindset and boost your overall well-being!

Meditation as a Tool for Mental Clarity

When your mind feels like it's spinning in a hundred different directions, meditation offers a way to press pause. It's not about emptying your mind or achieving perfection—it's about creating a calm, clear space where you can untangle your thoughts and reclaim your focus. Let's explore how meditation serves as a powerful tool for mental clarity, helping you manage overthinking and create a sense of inner peace.

At its core, meditation is a practice of calming the mind. Even just a few minutes a day can help clear the mental clutter that builds up from overthinking and stress. Research shows us that meditation has been shown to reduce anxiety, lower stress levels, and improve overall mental well-being (National Center for Complementary and Integrative Health, 2022). It works by promoting mindfulness, which helps you observe your thoughts with curiosity rather than getting caught up in them. This shift allows you to respond to challenges with clarity instead of reacting out of worry or fear.

Mindfulness, a cornerstone of meditation, is all about being fully present in the moment. When your thoughts start to race—analyzing the past or worrying about the future—mindfulness pulls you back to the here and now. By observing your thoughts without judgment, you gain a sense of control over them instead of letting them control you. Over time, practicing mindfulness can weaken the grip of anxious thinking, helping you step out of unproductive mental spirals and into a space of calm awareness.

Creating a Consistent Practice

Like any habit, meditation becomes most effective when practiced regularly. Setting aside a specific time each day, even if it's just five minutes, can help establish a routine. Having a dedicated space for meditation—a quiet corner or a comfy chair—can boost your focus and relaxation. Tracking your progress, whether through a journal or an app, can also motivate you to stick with it, giving you a sense of accomplishment as you build a practice that supports your mental clarity.

Meditation isn't about stopping your thoughts; it's about learning to manage them with grace. Incorporating meditation into your life allows you to develop a tool that not only calms your mind but also empowers you to manage overthinking with intention and confidence. In the exercise that follows, you'll be guided through ways to get started so you can begin reaping the benefits of this transformative practice.

Exercise: Simple Meditation Techniques for Beginners

Blending these simple meditation techniques into your daily life will let you cultivate a sense of mindfulness and resilience that helps combat negative thoughts and builds a greater sense of peace.

Start With Breathing Exercises

Begin your meditation journey with a simple breathing exercise like nostril breathing, which you can practice anywhere. Get cozy in a quiet space where you can choose to sit or lie down. Begin by closing your mouth gently and bringing your attention to your breath. Use your right thumb to block your right nostril and take a slow, deep breath in through your left nostril, filling your lungs completely. When you've fully inhaled, use your right ring finger to close your left nostril, then open the right nostril and exhale slowly. After exhaling, inhale through the right nostril, then close it with your thumb and exhale through the left nostril. Continue this alternating pattern for five minutes, focusing on the rhythm of your breath and the sensations it brings, allowing each inhale and exhale to foster relaxation and calmness (Cronkleton & Walters, 2023).

Explore Guided Meditation Apps

Consider downloading a guided meditation app to provide structure and support. Popular options like Headspace, Calm, or Insight Timer offer a range of meditation practices tailored for beginners (McCormick & Owens, 2024). Set aside a few minutes each day to explore different meditations, focusing on themes such as stress relief, self-compassion, or overcoming negative thoughts. Experiment with different lengths and styles to find what resonates with you.

Incorporate Visualization Techniques

Boost your meditation practice by incorporating visualizations. Find a quiet space and take a few deep breaths. Imagine a peaceful setting—like a serene beach or your favorite place in nature. Picture the colors, sounds, and sensations around you. As you immerse yourself in this scene, allow any negative thoughts to drift away, replaced by feelings of calm and positivity. Visualization can be a powerful tool to combat negativity and enhance focus.

Understand Mindfulness in Addressing Overthinking

Recognize the role of mindfulness in managing racing thoughts. When you find yourself spiraling into anxious thinking, take a moment to observe your thoughts without judgment. Sit quietly and become aware of your mental chatter. Acknowledge these thoughts, then gently guide your focus back to your breath or your chosen visualization. Mindfulness encourages acceptance and helps create distance from overwhelming thoughts.

Practice Presence

To create a sense of control over your mind, practice presence throughout your day. Incorporate mindfulness into everyday activities like eating, walking, or washing dishes. Focus fully on the experience at hand—notice the textures, flavors, and sounds. This practice can help ground you in the moment and reduce the tendency to overthink.

Create a Consistent Meditation Practice

To build and maintain your meditation habit, set aside a specific time each day for your practice. Choose a routine that works for you, whether it's in the morning, during your lunch break, or before bed. Consistency helps form a habit and deepens your practice.

Track Your Progress

Consider keeping a meditation journal to track your progress. Note the date, duration, and type of meditation you practiced, along with any insights or feelings you experienced during the session. Regularly reviewing your entries can motivate you to continue and help you identify patterns in your practice. Welcome the journey, and remember that each step contributes to your overall well-being!

You've taken a big step toward breaking free from the overthinking cycle by exploring tools like gratitude and meditation. These practices aren't just about calming your mind; they're about reclaiming your time, energy, and self-worth. The key is consistency and kindness to yourself. There's no "perfect" way to do this; the only wrong move is not trying.

In the next chapter, we'll go even further by diving into mindfulness and the art of living in the present moment. If overthinking keeps you tangled in the past or future, mindfulness will teach you how to ground yourself firmly in the here and now. Get ready to explore what it means to truly be present, embracing each moment with openness and curiosity. Because life isn't waiting for you to get it all figured out—it's happening right now, and you deserve to fully live it. Let's dive in.

Chapter 8:

Mindfulness and Living in the Present

Our brains love to drag us into the past or launch us into a future we can't control, leaving us stuck in a whirlwind of self-doubt and mental exhaustion.

All that second-guessing steals the one thing you do have—this moment. Mindfulness is your ticket to stepping off the overthinking hamster wheel and truly living your life. When you practice mindfulness, you learn to quiet that critical voice in your head, accept who you are right now, and stop assuming the world is waiting to critique your every move.

In this chapter, we'll explore how mindfulness can change your relationship with yourself. You'll discover simple, practical techniques to anchor your thoughts, build self-awareness, and find peace in the present moment. No judgment, no pressure—just small, powerful steps to help you reclaim your confidence, calm your mind, and remind yourself that you're freaking amazing.

Sunlight Visualization for Stress Relief

Can you picture yourself standing in a cozy, sunlit spot on a cool morning? The warmth of the sun slowly spreads across your skin, filling you with a sense of calm and grounding. That's the essence of sunlight visualization—creating a mental escape to tap into the soothing, healing power of light.

Sunlight visualization isn't just daydreaming; it's a tool to help your mind and body relax. By focusing on the warmth and brightness of sunlight, even in your imagination, you can create a mental sanctuary—a space where stress feels lighter and clarity comes more easily.

In the middle of a hectic day, when everything feels overwhelming, this visualization can be your pause button. It's a reminder that even when life feels stormy, there's a place of safety and warmth you can always return to within yourself.

What makes sunlight visualization so powerful is its ability to evoke a feeling of emotional security. That imagined light isn't just warmth on your skin—it's comfort for your mind, a symbol of hope, and a small step toward healing from self-doubt and negativity.

Exercise: Sunlight Visualization for Stress Relief

When you incorporate this sunlight visualization technique into your life, you create a powerful tool for reducing stress and enhancing your mood. Here's how.

Understanding Sunlight Visualization

Begin by exploring the concept of sunlight visualization. Visualizing sunlight is an effective technique for fostering relaxation and clarity. This practice can help create a mental space of calmness, making it a quick and accessible way to relieve stress during hectic moments. Think about how sunlight represents warmth and safety, serving as a soothing balm for your emotional well-being.

Creating Your Calm Space

Find a quiet space where you can sit comfortably, whether it's at home, in a park, or anywhere you feel at ease. Close your eyes and take a few deep breaths to help center yourself. Let go of any distractions and focus on the present moment.

Visualizing the Sunlight

Once you feel calm, begin the visualization:

- Imagine a bright, warm sunlight shining down upon you. Picture it radiating from above, enveloping you in a gentle glow.

- Feel the warmth of the sun on your skin. Visualize this light dissolving any tension or stress you're holding in your body. Let it travel from the top of your head down to your toes, warming and relaxing each part of you.

Fostering Warmth and Safety

As you continue to visualize, allow yourself to accept the feelings of safety and comfort that sunlight brings. Imagine it nurturing your spirit, washing away negative thoughts or worries. You're in a serene, calm environment—perhaps a sunny beach, a peaceful garden, or a lush meadow. Allow the beauty of this place to strengthen the sense of warmth and healing.

Breathing With the Sunlight

Incorporate your breath into your visualization. With each inhale, imagine drawing in the light and warmth of the Sun. Feel its energy fill your body. With each exhale, release any remaining tension or negativity. Allow the sunlight to cleanse your thoughts and emotions, leaving you rejuvenated and at peace.

Implementing the Technique Into Daily Routines

Aim to practice this sunlight visualization for a few minutes each day. Choose moments that feel right for you—when you wake up, during your lunch break, or before bedtime. The more consistently you practice, the more effective this technique will become.

A Reminder of Positivity

After completing your visualization, take a moment to reflect on how it felt. Carry the sense of warmth and calmness with you as you continue your day. You might consider keeping a Post-it note or a small image of the sun in a visible space as a reminder of the warmth and positivity that exist around you.

Reflect on Your Experience

After your visualization sessions, take a moment to journal about your feelings:

- What emotions came up during the exercise?

_____
_____
_____
_____
_____

- Did you notice any changes in your stress levels?

_____
_____
_____

Maintaining a record of your experiences can boost self-awareness and help reinforce the benefits of sunlight visualization.

Welcome the practice, and remember that this simple visualization can bring a sense of peace and warmth to your daily routine!

Benefits of Regular Practice

Like anything worth doing, sunlight visualization becomes even more powerful with regular practice. When you make this technique a part of your routine, you'll likely notice stress beginning to melt away more easily, leaving you with a brighter and more optimistic outlook on life. As your mind becomes accustomed to returning to this calming, light-filled space, those moments of chaos or self-doubt will lose their grip faster.

Beyond stress relief, regular visualization helps you develop mindfulness—a natural byproduct of focusing your thoughts on something soothing and positive. This mindfulness sharpens your self-awareness, making it easier to recognize and gently shift unhelpful patterns of self-talk or emotional reactions. Over time, you'll find yourself more connected to your feelings and more attuned to what you need to stay grounded and resilient.

Personal Reflection on the Experience

One of the most beautiful aspects of sunlight visualization is how deeply personal it can be. Taking time to reflect on how this practice feels for you is key. This can boost its effectiveness. Maybe you feel a sense of warmth that reminds you of happy memories or a peaceful energy that helps you let go of tension. Whatever your experience, reflecting on it allows you to make the visualization your own.

Answer the following:

- What images, sensations, or emotions does it stir?

_____
_____
_____
_____
_____

Remember, there's no right way to connect with this technique. As you explore it, don't be afraid to tweak it to suit your preferences. Perhaps you picture a specific place that brings you peace, or maybe the light carries a color or sensation unique to you. Your visualization is a tool, and personalizing it ensures it remains meaningful and effective. The more you practice and reflect, the deeper your connection to this calming technique will grow.

Noting Meditation Technique

Have you ever wished you could turn down the volume on the constant chatter in your head? That's where noting meditation comes in—a practice designed to help you step back from your thoughts instead of getting swept up in them. At its core, noting meditation is about acknowledging what arises in your mind—whether it's a thought, feeling, or sensation—and simply labeling it without judgment. For example, "Oh look, there's a bird." You notice it, you label it, and you let it fly right on by.

This technique works because it invites mindfulness into your mental space. Rather than wrestling with your thoughts or trying to push them away, you observe them with curiosity and neutrality. For instance, the thought of *I feel useless today* pops in. You notice it, you label it, and you let it fly right on by.

Over time, this habit of nonreactive awareness helps you see your thoughts for what they are: fleeting, temporary, and not necessarily reflective of who you are or what you need to do.

One of the most valuable aspects of noting meditation is its ability to create self-awareness. As you practice, you begin to notice patterns in your thinking—maybe a tendency to focus on worst-case scenarios or a habit of spiraling into self-doubt. Recognizing these patterns is the first step toward changing them.

Noting meditation isn't about fixing your thoughts; it's about learning to live alongside them without letting them control you. By simply naming what you experience—without adding layers of criticism or judgment—you create a space for peace and clarity to grow.

Exercise: Noting Meditation Technique

When you engage in the noting meditation technique, you develop a mindful approach to self-awareness that boosts your ability to acknowledge and understand your thoughts and feelings without judgment. Here's how.

Setting the Scene

Choose a comfortable space where you can sit quietly without distractions. This could be a comfortable spot on the couch, a peaceful spot in a park, or any place where you feel relaxed. Sit comfortably with your back straight but not stiff—feel free to cross your legs or rest your hands on your lap.

Establishing a Time Frame

Decide how long you'd like to practice today. If you're a beginner, start with just five minutes. You can gradually increase the duration as you become more comfortable with the practice.

Begin With Your Breath

Close your eyes and take a few deep breaths to ground yourself. Inhale deeply through your nose, allowing your lungs to fill completely, and then exhale slowly through your mouth. Repeat this a few times until you feel settled.

Start Noting

Now, shift your focus to your thoughts as they arise. As thoughts come to you—whether they're worries, distractions, or plans—simply note them without judgment. You can use a gentle labeling system, such as:

- thinking
- worrying
- planning
- feeling

Acknowledge the thought and let it go. Imagine each thought as a passing cloud (or a bird) in the sky—observe it, label it, and then allow it to drift away. This practice encourages you to create space between you and your thoughts, fostering a sense of detachment.

Recognize Patterns

As you continue this practice, pay attention to any recurring themes in your thoughts:

- Do you notice times when you often worry?

_____
_____
_____
_____
_____

- Are there specific feelings that arise regularly?

_____
_____
_____
_____
_____

Noticing these patterns is an essential part of developing greater self-awareness.

Adjusting the Practice

Feel free to adjust the noting meditation to fit your comfort levels and schedules. If labeling thoughts doesn't resonate with you, try simply acknowledging your thoughts or feelings as they arise. Experimentation is encouraged! You might find that certain environments, postures, or durations work better for you than others.

Concluding the Practice

After your timer goes off or you feel ready to conclude, take a moment to reflect on your experience. Slowly open your eyes and take a few deep breaths again. Consider journaling about the thoughts or feelings you noted during your practice, as well as any patterns you noticed.

Daily Integration

Aim to incorporate noting meditation into your daily routine. You can practice it once a day or whenever you feel the need to refocus and ground yourself. The more consistently you practice, the more benefits you'll experience.

Accept this journey of self-discovery, and enjoy the process of becoming more present in your daily life!

Benefits of Noting Meditation

Noting meditation offers a wealth of benefits for your mental and emotional well-being. One of its most powerful effects is its ability to reduce the intensity of overwhelming thoughts and emotions. By observing your inner world with neutrality, you create a buffer between yourself and your reactions, allowing you to process challenges with greater clarity and calm.

Regular practice of noting meditation also sharpens your concentration. As you focus on acknowledging and labeling your thoughts, your mind becomes more attuned to staying present—a skill that spills over into other areas of life, from work to relationships. This heightened focus contributes to improved overall mental health, reducing stress and fostering a more balanced outlook.

Perhaps most importantly, noting meditation nurtures a sense of peace and acceptance. Instead of battling your thoughts or feelings, you learn to coexist with them, building emotional resilience and a deeper understanding of yourself. Over time, this practice helps you respond to life's ups and downs with greater grace and steadiness.

Encouraging Regular Practice

To truly reap the benefits of noting meditation, consistency is key. Consider setting aside specific times each week to practice, whether it's first thing in the morning, during a lunch break, or as a way to wind down in the evening. Having a regular schedule makes it easier to turn this practice into a habit.

Creating a quiet, comfortable space for your meditation can also make a big difference. This doesn't mean you need a special room or fancy equipment—just a spot where you can sit, breathe, and focus without distractions.

If the idea of sitting in silence for too long feels overwhelming or uncomfortable, start small. Even a few minutes of noting meditation can have an impact. Gradually increase the duration as you grow more comfortable with the practice. The beauty of this technique is that it meets you where you are, inviting you to take things at your own pace while building a deeper connection with yourself.

By exploring mindfulness practices like sunlight visualization and noting meditation, you've taken meaningful steps toward calming your mind, quieting self-doubt, and building a stronger connection with yourself. These techniques aren't just tools for managing stress—they're invitations to live more fully in the present, to let go of what's holding you back, and to uncover the peace that's been within you all along.

In the next chapter, we'll dive into a topic that's both challenging and empowering: embracing vulnerability and authenticity. Together, we'll explore how letting down your walls and owning your true self can lead to deeper connections, greater confidence, and a life lived unapologetically. This one took me a beat to catch onto, but man, I am so glad I did. Get ready to unlock the courage to be real—it's the next step in becoming the bold, confident version of yourself that's been waiting to shine.

Chapter 9:

Embracing Vulnerability and Authenticity

Vulnerability can feel like walking into a room naked, knowing everyone else is fully dressed. It's uncomfortable, exposing, and downright terrifying at times. And yet, it's one of the most courageous things you can do. Why? Because vulnerability is where authenticity lives. It's where you stop pretending, stop filtering, and start showing up as you.

So, let's take a moment to imagine what life could look like if you stopped hiding behind perfectionism, fear of judgment, or that exhausting inner critic whispering, "You're not worthy of love." What if you could quiet that voice, lean into your true self, and trust that who you are, right now, is more than enough?

This chapter is your invitation to do just that. It's time to explore how accepting vulnerability opens the door to connection, confidence, and a sense of freedom you might not have felt in years. You'll learn how to show up authentically in your relationships, your work, and—most importantly—your relationship with yourself.

By the end of this chapter, you'll have real tools to embrace vulnerability and live authentically. You'll discover that the power to rewrite your story is already in your hands—and it starts with daring to be seen just as you are.

Exploring the Concept of Emotional Exposure

Vulnerability is often misunderstood. It's easy to think of it as exposing a weakness, as though being open about our struggles or fears will invite judgment or rejection. But vulnerability is bravery in action. It's the willingness to show up authentically, to remove the masks we wear, and to let others see us as we truly are. And yes, that can feel scary. But vulnerability is also the key to deeper connections, personal growth, and living an authentic life.

At its core, vulnerability is about openness and authenticity. It's the willingness to let others see the real you—the messy, imperfect, beautifully human you. When you accept vulnerability, you're saying, "This is who I am. I'm not perfect, but I'm enough."

And while it takes courage to show up in this way, vulnerability is a strength. It's what builds connection and growth. By opening yourself up, you allow others to truly know you, and that's where trust and intimacy begin. Vulnerability also paves the way for self-acceptance. When you stop trying to hide your flaws and start owning them, you free yourself from the exhausting need to please everyone else.

The Benefits of Vulnerability

Vulnerability can change everything in your relationships and personal well-being. When you let your guard down and share your true self, you create space for others to do the same. This shared openness builds trust and strengthens emotional bonds, making relationships more meaningful and resilient.

Being vulnerable also invites personal reflection and growth. When you acknowledge your fears and insecurities, you begin to understand yourself on a deeper level. This self-awareness is empowering—it helps you break free from the fear of judgment and live authentically.

Cultural Perspectives on Vulnerability

Unfortunately, societal norms often discourage vulnerability, portraying it as a sign of weakness. From an early age, we're taught to be strong, to hold it together, to never let others see us sweat. But these cultural narratives do more harm than good. They keep us stuck in a cycle of hiding our true selves, fearing rejection, and feeling disconnected.

The good news? You have the power to rewrite these beliefs. Consider re-evaluating how you view vulnerability. You can reclaim it as the strength it truly is. Recognizing and challenging harmful cultural narratives allows you to step into your authenticity and lean into the freedom it brings.

Sharing Personal Stories

One of the most powerful ways to embrace vulnerability is through storytelling. When you share your experiences—your struggles, your triumphs, your moments of doubt—you create a bridge of connection. You let others know they're not alone and, in turn, you invite them to share their own stories.

Authentic storytelling is about connecting with others and validating your own experiences and emotions. It's a reminder that your story matters and your voice has power. Sharing your journey creates community and inspires others to welcome their own vulnerability.

Exploring the concept of emotional exposure shows us that vulnerability is the path to a more connected, authentic life. It's not about being fearless but about showing up despite the fear.

Self-Acceptance Exercises to Build Confidence

Building confidence isn't about suddenly becoming fearless or never doubting yourself again—it's about learning to accept yourself as you are, flaws and all. It's about treating yourself with the same compassion and understanding you'd offer a close friend. When you pair self-acceptance with vulnerability, you create a powerful foundation for confidence, one rooted in authenticity and inner strength.

One of the most effective ways to build self-acceptance is through affirmations. These simple yet transformative statements are feel-good words and tools for reshaping how you see yourself and what you believe about your worth.

Affirmation Practices

Think of affirmations as a way to rewire your inner dialogue. If your mind tends to default to critical or negative self-talk, affirmations act like gentle reminders to focus on the positive. They can help you challenge unhelpful thoughts and replace them with ones that build you up rather than tear you down.

What makes affirmations truly impactful is how personal they are. The more an affirmation resonates with your experiences and aspirations, the more powerful it becomes. A generic "I am confident" might work for some, but for others, something more specific—like "I am proud of how far I've come, even if I'm still a work in progress"—can feel far more meaningful.

Consistency is the secret ingredient here. Affirmations aren't a quick fix but a practice that grows stronger over time. The more you use them, the more they begin to shape your thoughts and self-perception.

Why Affirmations Work

Affirmations help bridge the gap between vulnerability and confidence. By affirming your worth, you start to accept the parts of yourself you might otherwise shy away from. This acceptance allows you to show up authentically, without the need to hide behind perfectionism or fear of judgment.

When you integrate affirmations into your daily routine, they act as a compass, guiding you toward self-compassion, resilience, and belief in your own abilities. Over time, you'll notice how these simple phrases can quiet your inner critic and empower you to embrace the person you already are—flaws, strengths, and all.

Up next, we have a self-acceptance exercise designed to help you create affirmations that truly resonate with you. It's an opportunity to pause, reflect, and take a step toward embracing the incredible person you are.

Confidence isn't about perfection—it's about knowing you're enough, just as you are. And affirmations are one way to remind yourself of that truth every single day.

Exercise: Self-Acceptance Exercises to Build Confidence

Understanding Self-Acceptance

Before diving into the exercises, take a moment to reflect on what self-acceptance means to you. Acknowledge that embracing vulnerability is key to building confidence. It involves recognizing your strengths and weaknesses and understanding that both are part of your unique essence.

Create Personal Affirmations

Start crafting personal affirmations that promote self-love and acceptance. These statements should feel authentic and resonate with your experiences. Here's how to get started:

- **Identify areas of improvement:** Think about aspects of yourself that you often criticize or wish to change. Write them down.

_____
_____
_____
_____
_____

- **Reframe negativity:** For each area of improvement, reframe it into a positive affirmation. For example, if you often think, *I'm not creative*, flip it to, "I embrace my unique creativity and celebrate my ideas."

_____
_____
_____
_____
_____
_____
_____
_____

_____

_____

Customize Your Affirmations

Tailor your affirmations to reflect your personal experiences and struggles. This makes them more impactful and resonates on a deeper level. Here are some tailored examples:

- "I am worthy of love and respect just as I am."
- "I honor my journey and embrace my strengths and imperfections."
- "I am enough, and I choose to celebrate my uniqueness."

Daily Affirmation Practice

Incorporate your affirmations into your daily routine. Here are a few ways to make this practice consistent:

- **Morning ritual:** Recite your affirmations aloud each morning as part of your morning routine. Stand in front of a mirror, look into your eyes, and say the words with conviction.

- **Written affirmations:** Write your affirmations in a journal or on sticky notes placed around your home (e.g., on your bathroom mirror, computer, or fridge) so you see them throughout the day.

- **Affirmation apps:** Consider using apps designed for daily reminders of your affirmations, providing notifications to reinforce self-love during your busy day.

Track Your Progress

Keep a journal dedicated to your affirmation practice. Each week, write down your thoughts and feelings related to the affirmations. Reflect on any changes in your mindset—do you notice a shift in how you perceive yourself? Are you more aware of your strengths? Tracking your progress can enhance self-awareness and motivation.

Embrace Vulnerability

As you practice affirmations, recognize that being vulnerable is a strength. Consider moments when you felt vulnerable but also empowered. Write about these experiences, exploring how they contributed to your self-acceptance.

_____
_____
_____
_____
_____
_____
_____
_____
_____
_____
_____

Practice Self-Compassion

Alongside your affirmation practice, create self-compassion. When you notice negative self-talk creeping in, take a moment to pause and treat yourself with the same kindness you'd offer a friend. Remind yourself that everyone has insecurities, and it's okay to embrace yours.

Celebrate Your Journey

Take time to celebrate your efforts and successes in your journey toward self-acceptance. Whether it's small wins in your mindset or larger achievements in your life, acknowledging these moments reinforces your confidence and commitment to self-love.

When you engage in these self-acceptance exercises, you'll build a deeper sense of confidence and create a loving relationship with yourself. Welcome the process with patience and compassion, knowing that building self-acceptance is a beautiful path worth taking.

Exercise: Self-Compassion Techniques

Engaging in these self-compassion techniques lets you nurture a kinder relationship with yourself and build resilience against challenges and external judgment.

Understanding Self-Compassion

Before diving into the techniques, it's important to recognize what self-compassion truly means. Self-compassion involves treating yourself with kindness and understanding when you face challenges or make mistakes. It allows you to accept your vulnerabilities and be gentle with yourself, especially during difficult times. Remember, self-compassion is a powerful tool that increases your resilience against external judgment and promotes emotional well-being.

Kindness to Yourself

Start by practicing kindness toward yourself during moments of struggle. When you face a setback or feel overwhelmed, pause and acknowledge your feelings. Instead of criticizing yourself, say something kind. For example:

- "It's okay to feel this way; everyone struggles sometimes."
- "I'm doing the best I can in this moment."

The Self-Compassion Break

This technique is a simple yet effective way to practice self-compassion. Here's how to do it:

- **Recognize:** When you're feeling stressed or down, take a moment to recognize your feelings. Allow yourself to acknowledge what you're experiencing without judgment.
- **Connect:** Remind yourself that suffering and personal inadequacy are part of the shared human experience. You're not alone in feeling this way—many others have similar feelings.
- **Self-kindness:** Then, offer yourself a kind statement or affirmation. You might say, "May I be kind to myself in this moment" or "I deserve compassion just like anyone else."

Forgiving Yourself

To further build self-compassion, practice self-forgiveness. Identify a recent mistake or perceived failure and write about it. Consider the following:

- What did you learn from the experience?

___

- How can you treat yourself with understanding and kindness regarding that mistake?

___

- Write a letter to yourself as if you were comforting a friend, acknowledging your feelings and offering forgiveness.

___

Mindfulness Meditation

Incorporate mindfulness meditation into your routine. Allocate a few minutes each day to sit quietly and focus on your breath. As thoughts arise, gently acknowledge them without judgment, allowing them to pass like clouds. Visualize wrapping yourself in a blanket of kindness and warmth during this practice, letting self-compassion wash over you.

Develop a Self-Compassion Statement

Create a personal self-compassion statement that resonates with you. This can serve as a reminder to treat yourself kindly. For example:

- "I am enough, and it's okay to be imperfect."
- "I embrace my vulnerabilities as part of my journey."

Write this statement down so you can refer to it when needed.

Resilience Through Self-Compassion

Reflect on how practicing self-compassion can strengthen your resilience. When facing external judgment or criticism, remind yourself of your self-compassion techniques. Instead of internalizing negativity, use your compassionate tools to reinforce your self-worth. Journal about how you can respond to external judgments with kindness toward yourself.

Celebrate Your Efforts

Finally, celebrate your efforts to practice self-compassion. Keep a gratitude journal where you note moments when you treated yourself kindly or practiced forgiveness. Reflect on these moments as victories in your journey.

It's time to accept this adventure with an open heart, knowing that self-compassion is a vital aspect of building emotional well-being and inner strength!

Reflective Journaling

Journaling allows you to create a safe space to explore your emotions, beliefs, and experiences. It allows you to identify the emotional barriers standing between you and self-acceptance. Often, we carry stories about ourselves—narratives that say we're not good enough, smart enough, or lovable enough. Journaling gives you the opportunity to challenge those stories and rewrite them with a kinder, more compassionate lens.

Through reflection, you can uncover how vulnerability plays a role in your personal narrative. Try asking yourself the following:

- What fears or judgments hold you back from showing up authentically?

_____
_____
_____
_____
_____

- What moments in your life have taught you to shield your true self?

_____
_____
_____
_____
_____

When you explore these questions, you gain a deeper understanding of how your beliefs were formed and how they might be reframed to support growth and self-acceptance.

Writing also has a clarifying effect. Thoughts and feelings that feel tangled or overwhelming in your mind often become clearer on the page. This clarity creates room for acceptance and empowers you to move forward with a greater sense of peace and self-awareness.

Visualization: Seeing Yourself With Compassion

While journaling helps you reflect on your past and present, visualization allows you to imagine the future—a future where self-acceptance and confidence are your reality. Visualization is a tool to create mental images of how it feels to live authentically, free from self-doubt and fear of judgment.

Picture yourself standing confidently, speaking your truth, and embracing your imperfections. Think of positive scenarios where you handle challenges with grace and see yourself through a lens of compassion. By engaging your imagination in this way, you reinforce feelings of self-worth and begin to internalize the idea that you're enough, just as you are.

Visualization also creates a safe space to explore your true self. When you imagine a version of yourself that's fully accepted and embraced, you start to see the possibilities for making that version a reality. It's not about perfection but about stepping into the fullness of who you already are.

Both journaling and visualization work together to support self-acceptance by helping you understand and embrace your inner world. Journaling provides a space for reflection and insight, while visualization invites you to dream and believe in your potential.

These practices remind you that self-acceptance is a process. By engaging with your thoughts, feelings, and imagination, you take meaningful steps toward a life where vulnerability and authenticity become your greatest strengths.

Personal Reflection for Embracing Your True Self

Discovering and embracing your authentic self requires more than a surface-level glance in the mirror—it's about diving deep into your thoughts, beliefs, and values to uncover what truly makes you *you*. Reflection is the bridge that connects you to your true self, helping you untangle who you are from who the world might have told you to be.

One of the most powerful ways to begin this is by identifying your core values. These are the principles and beliefs that matter most to you, the ones that light you up and guide you toward what feels right and true. Core values are like a personal compass—they help you navigate decisions, align your actions with your authentic self, and steer clear of distractions that don't serve your goals.

Take a moment to consider what values are at the heart of your life. Maybe it's integrity, creativity, family, adventure, or kindness. Whatever they are, your values are uniquely yours, and they serve as a foundation for self-awareness and confidence. When you know what truly matters to you, it becomes easier to live in a way that feels genuine and fulfilling.

How Values Shape Authenticity

Understanding your values is a key step in embracing authenticity. When you're clear on what you stand for, you're less likely to be swayed by external influences or societal expectations. Instead of trying to fit into someone else's mold, you can confidently make choices that align with your inner truth.

For example, if authenticity and connection are core values for you, you might find it easier to set boundaries in relationships that don't honor those values. Or, if growth and learning are important to you, you'll likely seek opportunities that challenge and inspire you, even if they feel uncomfortable at first.

Reflecting on your values is also a powerful way to build self-acceptance. When you recognize the principles that guide you, you start to see yourself not as a collection of flaws and insecurities but as someone driven by meaningful ideals. This perspective can shift your focus from self-doubt to self-respect, empowering you to show up authentically in all areas of your life.

A Call to Reflection

Reflection isn't about finding the right values or proving anything to anyone—it's about understanding yourself better and using that understanding to live with intention. By taking the time to articulate your values, you create a road map to your authentic self, one that helps you stay grounded, confident, and true to who you are.

In the next section, we'll explore a reflective exercise to help you identify and connect with your core values. As you begin this practice, remember: Your values are already within you, waiting to be discovered. This is your opportunity to listen to your inner voice and let it guide you toward the life you're meant to live.

Exercise: Personal Reflection for Embracing Your True Self

Identifying Your Core Values

Take a moment to think about what truly matters in your life. Core values are the fundamental beliefs that guide your actions and decisions. To help articulate your personal values, consider the following steps:

- **List your values:** Write down any values that come to mind. Common examples include honesty, compassion, creativity, freedom, family, and growth.

_____

_____

_____

_____

_____

- **Prioritize your values:** From your list, identify your top three to five core values. These are the principles that resonate deeply with you and influence your life choices.

_____

_____

_____

_____

_____

- **Reflect on your values:** Write a few sentences about each core value. How do they shape your actions and decisions? How do they reinforce your sense of authenticity? This exercise will clarify how your values align with your true self.

_____
_____
_____
_____
_____
_____
_____
_____
_____
_____
_____

Understanding How Values Inform Authenticity

Reflect on how understanding your core values can help you align your actions with your authentic self. Ask yourself:

- In what ways do I currently honor my values in my daily life?

_____
_____
_____
_____
_____

- Are there aspects of my life where I feel disconnected from my values?

_____
_____
_____
_____
_____

- What changes can I make to align better with my true self?

_____
_____
_____
_____
_____

Reflective Questions for Deep Introspection

Now, let's dive into a series of reflective questions designed to encourage deep introspection about your identity and beliefs regarding vulnerability and authenticity:

- What does being true to myself mean to me?

_____
_____
_____
_____
_____

- What fears do I have about embracing my authentic self?

- How do I define vulnerability, and how comfortable am I with being vulnerable?

- In what situations do I feel most authentic and alive?

- Who in my life inspires me to be my true self, and why?

- Are there external influences (e.g., societal expectations, family beliefs) that impact my ability to express my authenticity? How can I lessen their influence?

- What strengths or qualities do I possess that I often overlook or undervalue?

Unearthing Hidden Fears and Desires

As you engage with these reflection questions, look for patterns in your answers. Write down any hidden fears or desires that surface and consider how they may have held you back from being your true self.

Recognizing Growth Opportunities

Take note of any insights you gain during this reflective process regarding your personal strengths and growth opportunities. Reflect on how you can continue nurturing these strengths and utilizing them to embrace your authentic self.

_____
_____
_____
_____
_____

Create an Action Plan

After completing your reflection, outline a plan for how you can further embrace your true self. This could involve:

- setting specific goals that align with your core values
- engaging in activities that foster authenticity, such as creative pursuits or connection with supportive communities
- seeking opportunities to practice vulnerability in safe spaces

_____
_____
_____

_____

_____

_____

_____

_____

_____

_____

Regular Check-Ins

Make it a habit to periodically revisit your core values and the insights you've gained through this reflection. Consider scheduling regular check-ins—perhaps monthly or quarterly—to assess your alignment with your authentic self and track your personal growth journey.

When you engage in this personal reflection exercise, you'll create a deeper understanding and acceptance of your true self. Accept the process, and remember that welcoming authenticity is a beautiful process worth pursuing!

Exploring Authenticity: Defining Your True Self

What does it really mean to be authentic? For each of us, authenticity looks and feels a little different. At its core, it's about self-acceptance and having the courage to show up in the world as your true self—unfiltered, unpolished, and unapologetically *you*. It's not about perfection or always getting it right; it's about honoring your values, emotions, and experiences without feeling the need to hide or perform for others.

Authenticity Starts With Self-Acceptance

Authenticity isn't something you become; it's something you embrace. To be authentic, you must first accept yourself as you are. This means letting go of the idea that you have to meet societal expectations or the perceived approval of others to feel worthy. It means acknowledging your strengths, imperfections, and everything in between—and knowing that all of it is what makes you whole.

But being authentic takes courage. It requires you to show up even when you're scared of judgment or rejection. It challenges you to peel back the layers of who you've been told to be so you can rediscover who you truly are. And that's no small feat.

Breaking Free From Barriers

Many of us face barriers to authenticity without even realizing it. These barriers often come from societal pressures to conform or fit into roles we've outgrown. They might sound like, "You have to be nice to be liked," or "Don't show weakness; people will take advantage of you."

Understanding these barriers is the first step toward breaking free from them. By identifying the beliefs and fears that hold you back, you can begin to question their validity. Do they truly reflect who you are, or are they just outdated stories you've been carrying around? The more you challenge these narratives, the more liberated you become to live authentically.

One of the most rewarding aspects of embracing authenticity is how it changes your relationships. When you show up as your true self, you invite others to do the same. Authenticity creates a ripple effect, fostering deeper trust, richer connections, and a sense of belonging. It allows you to connect with others based not on who you think you should be but on who you actually are.

The Role of Accountability Partners

As you walk the path to authenticity, having support can make all the difference. An accountability partner—a trusted friend, mentor, or even a therapist—can help you stay true to yourself when the going gets tough.

When you share your goals and vulnerabilities with someone who supports your growth, you create a culture of openness. This person can gently remind you of your values when self-doubt creeps in or when you're tempted to retreat behind old habits of inauthenticity.

Accountability partners also provide a safe space to discuss the challenges of being vulnerable and authentic. Their encouragement fosters your commitment to living truthfully, even when it feels uncomfortable.

I get it. Embracing vulnerability, exploring your true self, and breaking free from the barriers of societal expectations isn't easy. Believe me, I've been there. There were moments when I thought, *What if I'm not enough? What if I show the real me and it's a disaster—or worse, rejection?* But what I've learned along the way is this: Every step you take toward authenticity, no matter how small, brings you closer to a life that feels *real*.

The final chapter is all about creating lasting change. It's where the work you've done so far comes together and transforms into something tangible, something that carries you forward long after you close this book. You're going to take what you've uncovered about yourself—your values, your strengths, and yes, even your imperfections—and use it to build the life you want.

Chapter 10:

Creating Lasting Change

You've made it to the final chapter, and let me just say—look at you go! Seriously, take a second and appreciate the work you've already done. You've tackled the tough stuff, faced the mirror, and peeled back the layers of self-doubt that have been holding you hostage. That's no small feat, my friend. You've shown up for yourself, and that's a massive step toward building the life you deserve.

But real change—the kind that sticks—requires more than just those "aha" moments or breakthroughs. It's not about perfection (thankfully—because, let's be real, no one has time for that). It's about consistency, about showing up for yourself over and over, even when the initial excitement has faded. This is where the magic happens—when you blend self-care, self-respect, and self-belief into your everyday life.

In this chapter, we're going to shift gears from the "what" to the "how." How do you maintain this momentum? How do you stop those old habits of negative self-talk from sneaking back in? How do you protect the confidence you've worked so hard to rebuild?

You're not here for a quick fix or a feel-good moment that fades by next Tuesday. You're here to create lasting change—change that carries you through the messy days, the setbacks, and those moments when doubt tries to creep back in.

Let's get practical, let's get real, and, most importantly, let's make it doable. Because you're beautiful and capable, right now, exactly as you are. And from here on out, we're going to make sure you never forget that. Ready? Let's get started.

Setting Up Daily Self-Care Practices

Let's talk about routines—not the rigid, soul-sucking kind that make you feel like you're failing if you miss a step, but the gentle, supportive rhythms that nurture your mental and emotional health. Think of these routines as little anchors in your day, keeping you grounded no matter how wild life gets. Because, let's face it, the world can feel like a whirlwind, and self-care routines are your way of saying, "Hey, I've got me."

Morning Rituals: Starting Your Day With Purpose

Mornings can be magical—or chaotic, depending on how you approach them. Setting up an intentional morning ritual is like giving yourself a head start on the day. Even something simple, like taking five minutes to sip your coffee without distractions, can set a positive tone. Gratitude journaling, quiet reflection, or even just a moment to breathe deeply before diving into your to-do list can shift your mindset in ways you might not expect.

The beauty of a morning routine isn't in how elaborate it is—it's in how it makes you feel. It's your moment to claim a sense of control, to remind yourself that you're in charge of how you show up for the day. And when you start your day with intention, you're more likely to handle the curveballs with grace instead of frustration.

Evening Wind-Down: Finding Peace at Day's End

Evenings, on the other hand, are all about letting go. Your day is done, and you deserve to wrap it up with a little tenderness for yourself. Maybe it's a cup of tea, some light stretching, or simply dimming the lights and powering down your screens. These rituals signal to your body and mind that it's time to rest.

This is also the perfect time to reflect on your day. What went well? Maybe it's something big, like nailing a work presentation, or something small, like getting through the day without that voice of self-doubt taking over. Whatever it is, take a moment to acknowledge it. This kind of reflection isn't about perfection; it's about celebrating the effort, the wins, and the fact that you made it through.

When you treat your evenings as a time to unwind and recharge, you're not just prepping for better sleep—you're also reminding yourself that you deserve moments of calm.

Weekly Self-Care Check-Ins: Staying on Track

Now, let's zoom out a bit. While daily routines are vital, a weekly self-care check-in gives you the chance to step back and ask, "How am I doing?" This isn't about grading yourself or aiming for some kind of self-care perfection. It's about checking in with your emotional and physical needs. Are your routines helping, or do they need a little tweak?

Think of this as a conversation with yourself—a moment to reflect on what's working and what's not. Maybe you realize that gratitude journaling in the morning makes your day brighter, or maybe you notice that skipping your evening wind-down leaves you feeling frazzled. These check-ins keep you accountable and give you the chance to adjust your routines to fit your life, not the other way around.

Carving out time for these small but powerful practices sends a clear message to yourself: "I am worth this effort." And that's a message you can never repeat too often.

Exercise: Creating a Self-Care Tool Kit

Creating a self-care tool kit empowers you to prioritize your well-being in an enjoyable and meaningful way.

Understanding the Importance of a Self-Care Tool Kit

Let's start by discussing what a self-care tool kit is. This is a curated collection of resources, activities, and practices designed to support your well-being and recharge your spirit. Having a tool kit empowers you to choose what resonates with you on any given day, making it easier to prioritize self-care when you need it most. Plus, building a tool kit brings creativity to your self-care routine, enhancing its enjoyment and effectiveness.

Gather Your Tool Kit Essentials

Begin by selecting a container for your tool kit. It could be a physical box, a tote bag, or even a digital document—whatever feels right for you. The goal is to have a dedicated place to keep your self-care resources.

Identifying Activities and Resources

Consider the following categories to help you brainstorm various activities that foster joy, relaxation, and connection with yourself:

- **Relaxation practices:** Think about activities that calm and soothe you. Some ideas include:
    - deep breathing exercises or meditation apps
    - calming teas or aromatic candles
    - a soft blanket or a favorite pillow for cozy moments
- **Creativity boosters:** Engaging in creative pursuits can uplift your spirits. Ideas might include:
    - art supplies for drawing, painting, or coloring
    - craft materials for DIY projects
    - journals for writing, doodling, or gratitude lists
- **Physical well-being:** Incorporate activities that promote movement and wellness:
    - a yoga mat or workout video/channel
    - comfortable walking shoes for nature walks

- guided stretching routines or exercise playlists

- **Joyful connections:** Connect with yourself and others through meaningful activities:

    - a playlist of your favorite uplifting songs

    - books or podcasts that inspire you or make you laugh

    - a list of friends or loved ones to reach out to when you need a boost

Evaluating Your Resources

As you compile your list, evaluate which activities and resources resonate most with your needs and preferences. Ask yourself the following questions:

- Which activities do I genuinely enjoy and find enriching?

_____
_____
_____
_____
_____

- How do I feel after engaging in these activities?

_____
_____
_____
_____
_____

- Are there any new activities I've been curious to try?

_____
_____
_____
_____
_____

Building Your Tool Kit

Once you have a list of activities, start collecting or creating the items for your tool kit. Here are some easy ways to assemble your tool kit:

- Purchase or gather physical items based on your lists.

- Create a digital folder with links to online resources, like meditation guides or inspiring articles.

- Write down your favorite affirmations, quotes, or mantras and keep them handy.

Incorporate Variety

Aim for a diverse range of activities in your tool kit so you can choose something different depending on your mood. Having options allows you to adapt your self-care routine to what you need at the moment.

Regularly Update Your Tool Kit

Your self-care needs may change over time, so make it a habit to revisit and refresh your tool kit. Set aside time every few months to reflect on which activities still resonate and add new ones that excite you. This keeps your self-care routine dynamic and engaging.

Using Your Self-Care Tool Kit

When you find yourself needing a moment of self-care, reach for your tool kit! Choose an activity that resonates with you at that moment, whether it's reading, meditating, or engaging in a creative project. Allow yourself to enjoy the process without judgment.

Enjoy this process, and remember that self-care is about nourishing your mind, body, and spirit!

Understanding the Importance of Emotional Resilience

Life doesn't always play fair. You've probably had your share of tough days (or maybe entire seasons) when everything feels like too much. This is where emotional resilience comes in. Think of it as your inner bounce-back muscle—the thing that helps you face challenges, dust yourself off, and keep going even when it feels like the world is working against you.

Emotional resilience isn't about never feeling upset or stressed—it's about how you respond when those feelings inevitably show up. It's the ability to bounce back from setbacks and keep moving forward with a positive outlook, even when life gets messy.

When you cultivate resilience, you're essentially reinforcing your self-worth. You start to realize that no matter what life throws your way, you're capable of handling it. That's a powerful mindset shift—one that not only reduces stress but also helps you approach challenges with confidence instead of fear.

Benefits of Building Resilience

So, why is resilience such a big deal when it comes to self-care? For starters, resilient people tend to experience less anxiety and depression. That's because resilience acts like a buffer, helping you manage stress before it spirals out of control.

It also boosts your problem-solving skills, which means you're more likely to take proactive steps toward self-care rather than feeling stuck or overwhelmed. Resilience gives you the courage to reach out for support when you need it—whether that's from friends, family, or professionals. And let's not forget, a resilient mindset keeps you motivated to stick with those daily self-care routines, even when you're not feeling 100%.

Building Resilience: Practical Strategies

One way to start building resilience is by practicing self-reflection. When things don't go as planned, ask yourself: "What can I learn from this?"

Growth often comes from understanding your experiences, even the difficult ones.

Another cornerstone of resilience is connection. Building strong social relationships gives you a safety net to lean on when times get tough. Knowing you have people who support you can make all the difference.

And let's not forget about mindfulness—it's like a secret weapon for resilience. Staying present, focusing on your breath, or even just taking a mindful walk can help you stay grounded when stress starts to creep in.

Revisiting Resilience When Needed

Of course, resilience isn't a one-and-done kind of deal. There will be times when you feel emotionally drained or stretched too thin. That's okay—it's all part of being human. The key is to recognize those moments and take action.

If you're feeling emotionally fatigued, it might be a sign to revisit your self-care practices or even seek professional support. There's no shame in asking for help; in fact, it's one of the most resilient things you can do.

Emotional resilience isn't about never struggling—it's about knowing that struggles don't define you. It's about facing life's challenges with grace and grit, knowing that you have the tools to handle whatever comes your way. And that, my friend, is a superpower worth nurturing.

Exercises for Integrating Self-Care Into Everyday Life

Self-care doesn't have to be a grand gesture or an all-day affair (though if you want to book that spa day, I fully support it!). The real magic of self-care lies in the small, consistent actions you take every day. These exercises are about blending self-care into your life, making it as natural as brushing your teeth or scrolling through your favorite social feed.

Mindfulness Moments: Little Breathers, Big Impact

Let's say you're in the middle of a chaotic day, but instead of letting stress completely take over, you pause. You close your eyes, take a deep breath, and exhale slowly. In that one small moment, you've created space for yourself—a chance to reset.

These mindfulness moments are like tiny pit stops for your brain. They don't require a yoga mat or a quiet room (though those help too). It can be as simple as taking three deep breaths before responding to an email or spending 30 seconds noticing the warmth of your coffee mug in the morning.

The goal is presence. By checking in with yourself throughout the day, you stay connected to your feelings and needs, which is the foundation of self-care.

Five-Minute Daily Gratitude: A Boost for Your Mood

If you've ever rolled your eyes at the idea of a gratitude journal, hear me out—this practice works wonders. Dedicating just five minutes a day to gratitude can shift your mindset in ways that feel almost magical.

Start small. Maybe it's a sticky note on your desk where you jot down three things you're thankful for. It doesn't have to be deep or profound—anything from "I made it through Monday" to "The sun came out today" counts.

Gratitude isn't just about appreciating the big wins; it's about finding joy in the everyday moments. Over time, this practice becomes a collection of positivity you can look back on when you need a reminder that life has its bright spots, even on the hardest days.

Self-Care Commitments: A Promise to Yourself

Think of self-care commitments as little pinky promises to yourself. These are the non-negotiables—the things you do to remind yourself that your well-being matters.

For example, you might commit to drinking enough water, taking a 10-minute walk every afternoon, or reading a chapter of your favorite book before bed. The key is to make these commitments realistic and personal to you.

When you follow through on these promises, you're reinforcing your own worth. You're telling yourself, "I matter enough to prioritize my needs." And when was the last time you felt guilty about keeping a promise to someone else? Treat yourself with the same dedication.

Creating Community Support: Self-Care Together

Who says self-care has to be a solo act? Inviting friends or family to join you in your self-care journey not only makes it more fun but also strengthens your relationships.

Maybe it's a weekly walk with a friend, a virtual check-in to share gratitude lists, or a group challenge to try a new self-care activity. Having accountability partners helps keep you motivated, and there's something incredibly validating about knowing someone else is cheering you on.

Plus, self-care can be contagious. When you prioritize your well-being, you're setting an example for those around you, inspiring them to do the same. And that ripple effect? That's how we make the world a little kinder, one act of self-care at a time.

These exercises aren't about adding more to your plate—they're about creating small, meaningful shifts that fit seamlessly into your life. With each step, you're not just integrating self-care into your day; you're building a stronger, more resilient you. Because let's face it—you deserve nothing less.

You've reached the end of this chapter, but in reality, it's just the beginning of something incredible—a lifelong journey of prioritizing yourself. The tools and strategies you've explored here are about showing up for yourself in big ways and small, even when life gets messy—because it always does.

Think of self-care not as an obligation but as a gift—a way of reminding yourself every single day that you're worthy of time, effort, and love. Integrating mindfulness moments, gratitude practices, self-care commitments, and the support of your community allows you to create a foundation for lasting change. You're building resilience, nurturing your mental health, and setting the tone for a life where you're no longer running on empty.

So, take a deep breath, give yourself some credit for how far you've come, and keep moving forward. You don't need to do it all—you just need to do what feels right for you. Because when you show up for yourself, you open the door to becoming the best, most vibrant version of who you already are. And that, my friend, is a version worth celebrating every single day.

Conclusion

As you finish the last page, take a moment to pause and celebrate the incredible work you've done. You've embarked on a path that not only uncovers the roots of negative self-talk but also teaches you to identify and challenge your inner critic. This isn't just about reading words on a page; it's about real, tangible change in how you view yourself and the world around you.

Think back to when you first opened this book. The uncertainty, the doubt—it's something we all know too well. Yet here you are, having taken courageous steps toward rewriting your inner narrative. You've learned how to stop those critical voices from ruling your life and instead to fill your mind with thoughts that truly reflect who you are: wonderfully complex, beautifully flawed, and perfectly imperfect. Remember, every page turned is a step taken toward building unshakable self-esteem and embracing a confidence mindset.

Every struggle with self-doubt and insecurity has been met with determination and resilience. You now have the tools to overcome the fear of judgment and break free from the chains of overthinking. It hasn't always been easy—no process worth pursuing ever is—but you've shown up for yourself time and again. This commitment to your growth speaks volumes about your strength and tenacity. Each small victory is proof that you're capable of overcoming obstacles and transforming your life.

Your experiences have guided you into understanding mindfulness and living in the present moment. You've discovered the importance of grounding yourself amid chaos, allowing clarity and calmness to guide your actions and decisions. Embracing mindfulness is like planting seeds of peace within your soul, creating a calm connection between your mind and body. You've realized that true empowerment arises not from perfection but from grace, acceptance, and authenticity.

As you move forward, remember the importance of self-care. Nurture yourself, honor your needs, and create space for rejuvenation. By prioritizing self-care, you're affirming your own worth and reinforcing that you deserve love and care, just as much as you give to others. Don't wait until exhaustion creeps in to take care of you. Make it a daily practice, a promise to yourself that you'll be present for your own happiness and health. It's a beautiful act of self-love that fuels your journey ahead.

Accepting this path means understanding that progress isn't always a straight line. There will be highs and lows, moments when everything makes sense, and times when it feels confusing. Every little step forward is a victory worth celebrating. Try to find the beauty in these challenges as they help you grow and discover new things about yourself. Accepting this allows you to build resilience, realizing that healing is like a dance with yourself, full of twists, turns, and graceful moves.

Remember to continue to practice self-compassion. Be gentle with yourself, especially in tough times. We all face struggles, and we all deserve kindness and understanding. Self-compassion is like giving your soul a gentle hug, reminding you that it's okay to stumble and not have all the answers. This loving acceptance helps restore your spirit, giving you the strength to get back up and keep moving forward.

Commit to lifelong learning because personal development never stops. It's an ongoing, exciting adventure that can enrich your life in surprising ways. Stay curious, look for new insights, and broaden your understanding of yourself and the world around you. This will open up endless possibilities for growth, positively influencing your mindset and emotional well-being.

As we wrap up, take a moment to reflect on how far you've come and dream about where you can go next. Carry the knowledge, courage, and resilience you've gained; let them be your constant companions in whatever you pursue. Trust in your ability to face life's uncertainties, knowing you have the strength to handle whatever comes your way.

If this book has touched your heart, please think about leaving a review. Your feedback means so much, not just to me but to the many women looking for guidance on their own paths. Your words could help light the way for someone else, making sure this empowering content reaches those who need it most.

It's time to step confidently into the future, knowing you're enough just as you are. Celebrate, learn from your setbacks, and cherish the amazing person you're becoming every single day. Here's to you and your incredible life ahead!

Resources for Continued Growth

You've done the deep work, and now it's time to keep the momentum going. This resource page will be your go-to tool kit for all things self-care, resilience, and personal growth.

Support Groups and Communities

When you're exploring new communities, focus on finding ones that truly vibe with your needs and make you feel comfortable. Look for groups that radiate positivity, have clear and welcoming guidelines, and create a supportive, uplifting atmosphere.

- **Local community sites:** Consider the National Alliance on Mental Illness (NAMI), which offers free online resources and communities where you can connect and share resources with others. This site is perfect for finding reliable information and support.

- **Mental health apps:** Consider apps like Calm, Headspace, and BetterHelp, communities where users can connect, share progress, and support each other.

- **Social media groups:** Platforms like Facebook, Reddit, and LinkedIn have groups for specific interests, such as mental health, self-care, hobbies, or career growth. Just search keywords like "anxiety support" or "self-care practices" and join the group that fits your needs.

Mental Health Resources

Finding mental health resources can start with a few simple steps:

- **Therapy options:** To find a therapist, try directories like Psychology Today (psychologytoday.com) or Therapy for Black Girls (therapyforblackgirls.com). These sites let you search for therapists by location, specialty, and insurance. Many also offer virtual sessions for added flexibility.

- **Helplines:** Helplines provide immediate, confidential support. Here are some widely accessible options in the US:

    - **National Suicide Prevention Lifeline:** Call or text 988 for 24/7 crisis support.

    - **Crisis Text Line:** Text HOME to 741741 for free support in a mental health crisis.

    - **SAMHSA Helpline:** Call 1-800-662-HELP (4357) for assistance with substance abuse and mental health resources.

References

Abel, J. (n.d.). *How to silence your inner critic: Embrace it.* Jessica Abel. https://jessicaabel.com/silence-your-inner-critic/

Andersone, N. (2024, January 19). *Self-empowerment strategies for softening the inner critic.* Psychology Today. https://www.psychologytoday.com/intl/blog/human-inner-dynamics/202401/self-empowerment-strategies-for-softening-the-inner-critic

Bellingham, R. (2024, September 14). *Confidence and competence.* Perspectives & Possibilities. https://rickbellingham.com/2024/09/14/confidence-and-competence/

Building resilience and self-esteem: A powerful combination. (2023, April 26). Fearless. https://fearless.org.au/2023/04/26/building-resilience-and-self-esteem/

Cascio, C. N., O'Donnell, M. B., Tinney, F. J., Lieberman, M. D., Taylor, S. E., Strecher, V. J., & Falk, E. B. (2016). Self-affirmation activates brain systems associated with self-related processing and reward and is reinforced by future orientation. *Social Cognitive and Affective Neuroscience, 11*(4), 621–629. https://doi.org/10.1093/scan/nsv136

Cook, J. M., Simiola, V., McCarthy, E., Ellis, A., & Stirman, S. W. (2018). Use of reflective journaling to understand decision making regarding two evidence-based psychotherapies for PTSD:

Practice implications. *Practice Innovations*, *3*(3), 153–167. https://doi.org/10.1037/pri0000070

Cooks-Campbell, A. (2023, November 28). Triggered? Learn what emotional triggers are and how to deal with them. *BetterUp*. https://www.betterup.com/blog/triggers

Cronkleton, E., & Walters, O. (2023, May 24). *What are the benefits and risks of alternate nostril breathing?* Healthline. https://www.healthline.com/health/alternate-nostril-breathing

Diniz, G., Korkes, L., Schiliró Tristão, L., Pelegrini, R., Lacerda Bellodi, P. L., & Bernardo, W. M. (2023). The effects of gratitude interventions: A systematic review and meta-analysis. *einstein (São Paulo)*, *21*, eRW0371. https://doi.org/10.31744/einstein_journal/2023rw0371

Elsesser, K. (2020, October 2). *The debate on power posing continues: Here's where we stand.* Forbes. https://www.forbes.com/sites/kimelsesser/2020/10/02/the-debate-on-power-posing-continues-heres-where-we-stand/

Expert Panel, Forbes Communications Council. (2024, August 12). *12 benefits of embracing vulnerability in leadership.* Forbes. https://www.forbes.com/councils/forbescommunicationscouncil/2020/03/02/12-benefits-of-embracing-vulnerability-in-leadership/

Grzybowski, J., & Brinthaupt, T. M. (2022). Trait mindfulness, self-compassion, and self-talk: A correlational analysis of young adults. *Behavioral Sciences*, *12*(9), 300. https://doi.org/10.3390/bs12090300

Guinness, H. (2024, July 10). The 5 best habit tracker apps in 2024. *Zapier.* https://zapier.com/blog/best-habit-tracker-app/

Gupta, S. (2023, May 25). *The importance of self-reflection: How looking inward can improve your mental health.* Verywell Mind. https://www.verywellmind.com/self-reflection-importance-benefits-and-strategies-7500858

Hutchinson, A. (2024, October 9). *How meditation can combat mental fatigue and supercharge your endurance.* Outside. https://www.outsideonline.com/health/training-performance/mindfulness-endurance-performance/

Kimmel, M. (2024, September 25). *Reframing negative thoughts-the power of positive thinking.* LinkedIn. https://www.linkedin.com/pulse/reframing-negative-thoughts-the-power-positive-meredith-kimmel-pcc-iphae

Maiocchi, M. (2022, March 20). *The visualization of the sun.* Spirit of Change. https://www.spiritofchange.org/the-visualization-of-the-sun/

Mayo Clinic Staff. (2023, November 21). *Positive thinking: Stop negative self-talk to reduce stress.* Mayo Clinic. https://www.mayoclinic.org/healthy-lifestyle/stress-management/in-depth/positive-thinking/art-20043950

McCormick, A., & Owens, H. (2024, November 12). *The 7 best meditation apps of 2024.* Verywell Mind.

https://www.verywellmind.com/best-meditation-apps-4767322

Miles, M. (2023, May 2). Power poses: How to feel more confident with body language. *BetterUp.* https://www.betterup.com/blog/power-poses

National Center for Complementary and Integrative Health. (2022, June). *Meditation and mindfulness: Effectiveness and safety.* https://www.nccih.nih.gov/health/meditation-and-mindfulness-effectiveness-and-safety

Negative self-talk: 8 ways to quiet your inner critic. (n.d.). *Calm.* https://www.calm.com/blog/negative-self-talk

Perez, C. (2023, October 6). *I write in a gratitude journal every day, here are all the benefits.* Vogue. https://www.vogue.com/article/gratitude-journal

The power of journaling for well-being: A path to self-discovery and healing. (2023, October 11). *Duke Health & Well-Being Blog.* https://dhwblog.dukehealth.org/the-power-of-journaling-for-well-being-a-path-to-self-discovery-and-healing/

Puddicombe, A. (2023, October 10). *What is the meditation noting technique and how to use it.* Headspace. https://www.headspace.com/articles/noting-technique-take-advantage

Rathor, R. (2023, November 12). *The art of goal visualization: Seeing success before it happens.* Medium. https://medium.com/@ruchirathor_23436/the-art-of-goal-visualization-seeing-success-before-it-happens-d571774e79a3

Red Top Wellness Center. (2024, June 2). *Overcoming negative self-talk: Strategies for a positive mindset.* https://www.redtopwellness.com/

blog/2024/june/overcoming-negative-self-talk-strategies-for-a-p/

Schaffner, A. K. (2024, November 15). *Living with the inner critic: 8 helpful worksheets.* PositivePsychology.com. https://positivepsychology.com/inner-critic-worksheets/

The Speaker Lab. (2024, June 23). 12 simple exercises to build confidence in any situation. *The Speaker Lab.* https://thespeakerlab.com/blog/confidence-building-exercises/

Sutton, J. (2024, December 18). *5 benefits of journaling for mental health.* PositivePsychology.com. https://positivepsychology.com/benefits-of-journaling/

Thorpe, M., & Ajmera, R. (2024, August 15). *How meditation benefits your mind and body.* Healthline. https://www.healthline.com/nutrition/12-benefits-of-meditation

Tull, M. (2023, December 6). *How to identify and cope with your PTSD triggers.* Verywell Mind. https://www.verywellmind.com/ptsd-triggers-and-coping-strategies-2797557

UCLA Health. (2023, March 22). *Health benefits of gratitude.* https://www.uclahealth.org/news/article/health-benefits-gratitude

Valenti, L. (2021, April 29). Visualisation to relate to the inner critic creatively. *Elemental Soul Medicine.*

https://www.elementalsoulmedicine.com/blog/visualisation-for-the-inner-critic/

Webb Wright, K. (2023a, May 4). Reflective journal: Inspiration, ideas, and prompts. *Day One*. https://dayoneapp.com/blog/reflective-journal/

Webb Wright, K. (2023b, November 2). Building self-awareness: How to use journaling to know yourself better. *Day One*. https://dayoneapp.com/blog/self-awareness/

Weineck, F., Schultchen, D., Hauke, G., Messner, M., & Pollatos, O. (2020). Using bodily postures to reduce anxiety and improve interoception: A comparison between powerful and neutral poses. *PloS One, 15*(12). https://doi.org/10.1371/journal.pone.0242578

Made in United States
North Haven, CT
09 August 2025